THE
ULTIMATE
MICRO-RPG
BOOK

40 Fast, Easy, and Fun Tabletop Games

EDITED BY JAMES D'AMATO

Author of *The Ultimate RPG Character Backstory Guide*

ADAMS MEDIA

NEW YORK   LONDON   TORONTO   SYDNEY   NEW DELHI

Adams Media
An Imprint of Simon & Schuster, Inc.
100 Technology Center Drive
Stoughton, MA 02072

First Adams Media trade paperback edition November 2020

ADAMS MEDIA and colophon are trademarks of Simon & Schuster.

For information about special discounts for bulk purchases, please contact Simon & Schuster Special Sales at 1-866-506-1949 or business@simonandschuster.com.

The Simon & Schuster Speakers Bureau can bring authors to your live event. For more information or to book an event contact the Simon & Schuster Speakers Bureau at 1-866-248-3049 or visit our website at www.simonspeakers.com.

Interior design by Colleen Cunningham, Erin Alexander, Priscilla Yuen, and Julia Jacintho
Images © 123RF; Getty Images

Manufactured in China

10 9 8 7 6 5 4 3

Library of Congress Cataloging-in-Publication Data
Names: D'Amato, James, editor.
Title: The ultimate micro-RPG book / edited by James D'Amato, author of The Ultimate RPG Character Backstory Guide.
Description: Avon, Massachusetts: Adams Media, 2020.
Series: The ultimate RPG guide series.
Identifiers: LCCN 2020018054 | ISBN 9781507212868 (pb) | ISBN 9781507212875 (ebook)
Subjects: LCSH: Fantasy games.
Classification: LCC GV1469.6 .U58 2020 | DDC 793.93--dc23
LC record available at https://lccn.loc.gov/2020018054

ISBN 978-1-5072-1286-8
ISBN 978-1-5072-1287-5 (ebook)

CONTENTS

INTRODUCTION

Welcome to the world of micro-role-playing games! Whether you'd like to brave the desolated landscape of an alien world, tell stories of high-paced medical drama, or even compete with one another in a break room at work to see who'll get sent home early, there's something for you here.

Since their invention in the 1970s, RPGs have entranced millions upon millions of players. *The Ultimate Micro-RPG Book* explores an exciting subset of this hobby. Whether you are new to the world of RPGs, or if you've been playing them for years, this book offers something for you. Many of the micro-games you'll find here are innovative, vastly different from anything you've played. Others are more traditional and are a great way to break into role-playing games.

This is a collection of forty tabletop role-playing games, ranging from fantasy to horror to humor. Each game has everything you need to make characters, build a world, and start playing, all in about two pages per game. The pages are designed to be torn out of the book, so you can have them for easy reference. The games' rules systems are explained in under a thousand words, so they won't take much time to learn. They don't take that long to play, either—usually about 1–3 hours.

Above all, micro-RPGs are about storytelling. You and your fellow gamers tell stories; where you go with them is up to you. Because of the compressed nature of micro-RPGs, the events of the resulting stories are few, but the range is as wide as the players want. In the following How to Use This Book section, you'll learn more about storytelling technique within RPGs and how to make your experience even more fun. This section will explain the general rules of micro-RPGs, how they're structured, and more. If you're an experienced RPG player, you may want to skip the first part of this section; however, if this is your first time playing RPGs, this will help you understand how to play them and what to expect.

Let the stories begin! There are worlds for you to explore!

HOW TO USE THIS BOOK

In this section you'll learn some basic techniques for role-playing. You'll also learn about establishing a safe and friendly atmosphere for your game, ensuring that all the players feel comfortable and can enjoy the game equally. Finally, you'll learn how the games in this book are set up and how you can identify which games will best suit you.

First of all, just what is an RPG? A **role-playing game (RPG)** is a type of game in which players generate fiction through shared imagination. The core concept behind RPGs is similar to imagination-based games people play when they are young, like "house," using dolls or action figures, and other simple games of pretend. These types of games call on players to inhabit a role and interact through shared imagination.

"Tabletop" RPGs published in game manuals introduce structure to this process. Published RPGs, or **role-playing systems**, help players establish goals, track abstract information, and resolve conflicts. Rule systems and randomizers (such as dice or cards) help adults make sense of what comes naturally to most children.

You might already be familiar with some well-known RPGs such as *Dungeons & Dragons*. When most people think of RPGs, they picture sword and sorcery stories told with polyhedral dice. However, RPGs have grown well beyond these roots to encompass every genre and set of mechanics imaginable. In this book you'll find games featuring horror, science fiction, romance, comedy, and so much more. The rules will call for dice, cards, handwritten notes, drawing maps, and even drawing temporary tattoos on each other's bodies!

It's a celebration of all the many wonderful things role-playing can be. Hopefully this book will help you discover a new passion, or at least a new way to enjoy something you already love.

WHAT IS A MICRO-RPG?

A **micro-RPG** is a role-playing game with rules that are no longer than a few pages. They can be as short as 100–200 words. There is no true defining factor for micro-games beyond their size, though they are typically grounded in specific scenarios or concepts. Like haiku or flash fiction they find boundless opportunities for creativity within limited space.

Designers of all experience levels use micro-RPGs to explore new mechanics, experiment with fresh game concepts, or simply create games that wouldn't work on a larger scale. While small games have existed since the early days of RPGs with photocopied ashcans and game zines being sold and passed around at conventions, the advent of online publishing has made micro-games a staple of modern design.

In the past, micro-RPGs have had something of an ephemeral quality, appearing at specific events, getting buried in forums, or getting lost in a sea of creative brilliance as they vie for attention against more polished-looking projects. This book collects innovative games created by veteran and new designers to bring you an exciting cross section of what is possible in the world of micro-design.

KNOWING THE ROLES

The games you'll find in this book have specific structural roles that work to make the game function. All the games have **player characters (PCs)**, and many—though not all—have **game masters (GMs)**. Although technically everyone involved in an RPG is playing the game and is therefore a "player," player characters are sometimes simply called "players."

What Is a PC?

In most of the games in this book, the players are responsible for controlling individual characters. For our purposes these characters and the people who play them are both called PCs.

Narratively, PCs are the protagonists, and players in the PC role are the primary authors of their story. PC players choose how their character thinks, looks, and acts. PCs interact with outside forces like other players and randomization, so a player in a PC role can't control everything that happens to their character. However, a PC player always controls how their character reacts to what happens.

Players in the PC role can have the following responsibilities:

- Determining their character's appearance, behavior, personality, and history
- Making decisions about their character's actions
- Embodying a character's voice
- Managing their character's statistics and abilities
- Addressing storytelling challenges through character action

These responsibilities and the overall function of this role can vary from game to game.

In some games, the most important aspects of a PC are the numbers, determined through various means like rolling dice and spending build points; however, not all games use dice to assign values in character creation, even within this collection, that make up their vital statistics. Others call for players to pay attention to their character's emotional state based on events in the game.

TIPS FOR BEING A GOOD PC

- **Be a fan of your character!** Root for your party and let them become your heroes.
- **Listen to your group!** RPGs are about collaboration, and your next great idea is probably in supporting someone's last great idea.
- **Chase your fun!** Don't be afraid to ask for things you want to see in the game.
- **Be experimental!** RPGs offer a chance to step outside everyday experiences, so swing for the fences.

What Is a GM?

Many RPGs, including the micro-RPGs in this book, have a specialized role that controls any elements of the game that are not PCs. The title for this role varies, but here we'll refer to it as the game master (GM).

The GM is like a narrator, director, producer, supporting actor, and crew rolled into one person. Colloquially we say GMs "run" the game. The GM is usually also the arbiter of a game's rules. Sometimes there are no clear rules in a game system for what's happening in the game scenario; sometimes there are a few contradictory rules that might apply. The GM is tasked with deciding what to do in those situations. The GM is also role-playing. They control the actions of **nonplayer characters (NPCs)**: characters that are not controlled by players, which function to support or oppose PCs in the story.

- **Be a fan of the PCs!** Even if you control the game's challenges, you are playing with the group, not against them.
- **Be a spotlight!** This is a story where the PCs are the protagonists; even if it's destined for tragedy, you want to set them up to look good.
- **Listen first!** Players spend the whole game telling you what they find interesting and tossing around good ideas—it's up to you to hear them.
- **Ask questions!** It's easier to move a story forward if you are answering a specific question than if you are creating in a vacuum. If your group gets stuck, look for the questions you are trying to answer.

Players in the GM role can have the following responsibilities:

- Determining the appearance, behavior, and personality of NPCs
- Controlling forces in the game world unrelated to characters, like environment and time
- Controlling the general flow and focus of the overall narrative
- Presenting PCs with challenges that advance their story
- Preparing materials for game sessions
- Understanding the rules of the game and deciding when they apply

The number and variety of responsibilities a GM role has varies based on game system and personal style.

> **By Any Other Name**
>
> Sometimes game designers pick different names to describe a player in the GM role. Usually it's to add some thematic flare to the game. The most important thing about a GM is what they do, not what they are called.

THE GOLDEN RULES

No matter what role you choose, there are three rules every player should follow. They'll make each game safe, fun, and rewarding.

1. People Matter More Than Games

RPGs are great, and it's really fun to get invested in your ideas and stories. However, that should never overshadow the real people you're sharing the table with. No one should ever have to swallow discomfort or compromise their feelings for the sake of a game.

Always remember to treat sensitive subjects with care, check in with your group as you play, and be willing to stop the game and start a conversation if people seem uncomfortable. Remember this also extends to yourself. No one at the table is more in touch with your feelings than you! You are your own best ally when it comes to caring for your well-being.

2. Fun Matters More Than Rules

RPGs are a truly infinite canvas—anything is possible within the realm of imagination, which means that the rules of a game can occasionally be a limitation. Ideally the rules funnel your creativity, reinforce themes, and provide interesting challenges. However, a designer can't anticipate every situation for every group. Sometimes the most obviously fun thing for everyone at the table goes beyond or counter to the rules of the game.

RPGs are less rigid than most other games. Because they are so intimately controlled by the players, they can accommodate bending or breaking a rule in the name of fun. This sort of decision works best if it's acknowledged and discussed in the open. Breaking rules and not telling anyone is cheating. Breaking rules as part of a group is working together to have a good time.

Generally speaking, if you and your fellow players think something is fun, you should do it!

3. Make Choices Important

The final rule is a twist on an old improv classic. If you know anything about improv, there's a good chance you've heard of the rule of "yes and." Essentially "yes and" is the basic cornerstone of collaboration. It's about embracing the ideas of the people you are working with, then building upon them.

Also, saying yes to an idea doesn't necessarily mean saying yes in character. Saying yes is merely accepting the proposed reality.

We prefer a slight twist on this rule: Make choices important. This rule challenges you to look at and build on the ideas of your fellow players in a specific way. First, it calls for you to view everything that happens at the table as an intentional choice that people are making. That assumes intention behind their ideas. Then it asks you to add to those ideas in a way that honors them and gives them personal significance by "making choices important."

The second is that it incorporates the idea of challenging material and a way to avoid it into the social contract of the game. If a player uses the X-Card, they are not being picky or difficult—they are playing by the rules. With this tool, there is an established protocol to be considerate of each other's comfort.

PROS
- Streamlines communication
- Easy to learn
- Noninvasive

CONS
- Reactive, not preventive
- Still requires someone to communicate in a difficult moment

EXAMPLE

Kimya: *You get home and your parents are talking in hushed tones about a sick relative. They seem tense.*

Ali: *I'm tapping X on this. I don't want to deal with serious illness.*

Kimya: *No worries! They are watching the news and appear to be on edge about what's happening.*

You can find additional information at http://tinyurl.com/x-card-rpg.

Lines and Veils

The system of lines and veils was developed by Emily Care Boss from concepts in *Sorcery & Sex* by Ron Edwards to facilitate players identifying difficult topics and to establish limits before a game starts. Players start by discussing the general themes of their game and point out specific subjects they feel sensitive about. A **line** is a hard content limit that indicates a player does not wish to encounter a subject in any form. A **veil** is more of a warning or indicator that a subject should be treated carefully and implied rather than directly narrated.

This allows everyone to proactively avoid situations that might trigger the use of a tool like an X-Card. It saves people the stress of accidentally upsetting their friends. It also helps players create a common understanding of their game's themes.

Just like with the X-Card, you never need to ask why a player requires a certain safety tool. Players are at the table to play, not to justify their trauma or taste. The only follow-up questions people should ask are ones that help clarify what content to avoid and how to avoid it.

PROS
- Informs people before a problem arises
- Affects play in an unobtrusive way

CONS
- Asks players to proactively identify their triggers
- Sometimes people don't discover difficulty until they are in the moment

Script Change

One of the most robust safety mechanics was created by one of the designers who contributed to this collection! Brie Beau Sheldon's **Script Change** is a set of tools to help a group establish a shared sense of tone and to control the action of a game when things get tricky.

Before the game starts, Script Change asks players to discuss a content "rating" that everyone would be familiar with, like those in films, TV shows, or video games.

This is a good starting reference point and puts players in the mind-set of people controlling a production.

During the game players place cards with **rewind**, **pause**, and **fast-forward** symbols on the table. The **rewind** card is similar to the X-Card. When a player encounters something they don't want in the game, they can tap or hold up "rewind" to move the story back to the point before that content was introduced and discuss alternative possibilities.

The **pause** card is used to facilitate conversation and indicate that a situation might call for greater context or care. After someone taps "pause," players cease narration and discuss upcoming events—or something that just happened—so everyone can be aware that the pausing player has additional needs to play comfortably. Pausing doesn't alter the scene like "rewind," but it fosters a meta conversation and brings focus back to the players rather than the game.

Finally, **fast-forward** indicates a need to move events past the current scene. Rather than taking a specific topic out of the game entirely, it changes how that topic or events are experienced. It signals to the group that a player is fine with what is happening, but they don't necessarily want to spend time watching it unfold.

These tools help establish the game as a controllable thing. Whether you are a PC or a GM, Script Change gives you agency. It also opens you up to the idea of applying tools that people use in other media to make you feel more at ease when role-playing.

- Provides lots of options for approaching difficult content
- Treats content more fluidly, making necessary changes easier

CONS

- More tools for players to learn makes setup take longer

You can find additional information at http://briebeau.com/thoughty/script-change/.

STATS BOX

In this book, we've made it easy to find the kind of game that's best suited to your mood, level of complexity, and playing time. Each entry has a Stats box—a handy graphic with basic information that will help you choose the perfect RPG for your group. For example:

> **Number of players:** 2–8
>
> **Playing time:** 2–4 hours
>
> **Complexity:** 1
>
> **You'll need:** 1 or more d6.
>
> **Goal:** To plan the greatest party in the galaxy.
>
> **Tags:**
>
> Genre: Science Fiction
>
> Tone: Funny
>
> Format: GMless
>
> Content: Whimsical, farcical, weird alien stuff

Here's what all this means:

Number of Players: Most of the games in our collection can easily accommodate groups from 3–6. Some are designed to be an intimate experience for just two players, and a few can be played alone!

Playing Time: Most of the games in this collection can be played in 1–3 hours. There are even some that will give you a satisfying experience in 30 minutes. Games vary in length due to the number of players, so assume a longer playing time with a larger group.

Complexity: This collection has games for people who are new to RPGs and folks who have been playing for decades. We rate our games on a scale of 1 to 4. Games at a 1 are very simple and easy to understand. Games at a 4 have more complex mechanics and might be more suited to experienced groups.

You'll Need: While our book gives you all the rules you need to play, some games require accessories like pens, paper, dice, playing cards, and even paint. This section lists everything you need to get started.

Goal: This is a simple one- to two-sentence description of what players are trying to accomplish during a game. It will help you focus and give you an idea of what a game is like.

Tags

This book contains forty games! Since we don't want you and your friends to have to read all of them just to know what you want to play, we've put together a system of tags so you can learn about our games at a glance and pick one that's just right for your group!

Genre

For some players, a game's setting is a huge part of the appeal. Sometimes you're in the mood for orcs and elves, sometimes you want to take a ship into deep space, and other times you just want to make the real world a little different. The Genre tags will give you a general idea of each game's setting so you can find just the right one.

Fantasy: Perhaps the most iconic setting for RPGs, fantasy games are set in worlds with elements of magic and the supernatural. When discussing the fantasy genre, most folks think of sword and sorcery stories like The Lord of the Rings or *Conan the Barbarian*. However, the genre can be more expansive than that; a fantasy story can be set in a modern urban area where monsters roam metropolitan streets. They can also have no magic at all and just take place in a world unlike our own.

In this collection, the Fantasy tag means the game will include swords, magic, monsters, a pseudo-medieval time period, or all of the above.

Science Fiction: The science fiction genre fills the world with wondrous technology and as-of-yet unseen discoveries. Sometimes science fiction looks far into the future; sometimes it makes the modern world unrecognizable with a small speculative push.

In this collection we have a particular affinity for outer space. If you like the idea of strange machines, robots, aliens, and the world of tomorrow, check out the Science Fiction tag.

Modern: Sometimes you want to play in a world that resembles our own. Games in the modern genre thrive on finding fun and adventure in the mundane or familiar. Modern games wear their differences on their sleeve and ask their audience to assume that pretty much everything else is the same as you would find in our world. If there is any magic or other element of the fantastic, it's probably presented as magical realism.

Horror: This genre focuses on the grim, macabre, and violent. Like many other genres, horror contains multitudes and means different things to different players. To some horror is about aesthetics—ghosts, monsters, and spooky locations. For others it's a signifier of subject matter—violence, powerlessness, and suspense. No matter what, you can expect a game tagged with the Horror tag to deal with conceptually scary things. It's always good to check in with your group about how intense you want your exploration of horror tropes to be.

Animals: In this collection we found our own genre of animal games, in which all or some of the players control animal characters. One of the true joys of role-playing is imagining an experience you could not possibly have in real life. Whether you play these games with grounded realism or over-the-top anthropomorphic intelligence, playing an animal gives you an opportunity to truly be different.

Most of our animal-themed games are farcical, so look for the Animal tag if you want to have wild fun.

Tone

Most of the time individual groups of players set the tone for their own games. However, depending on the setting and mechanics, a game can push you in a certain direction. The following tags describe what we expect will happen with most groups.

Adventurous: This is almost the default setting for RPGs. Games with an adventurous tone want you to seriously engage with their premise, but allow you to make it into what you want. They're not built to make you laugh or cry; they are built to engage your creativity and help you have fun. This means the tone of these games is the most variable depending on the group.

Games like *Pyrewaltz* and *Gnomesteaders* thrive on player energy and work best when everyone is fully invested, even if that takes you over the top.

Funny: These games are structured for jokes. They'll provide the perfect setups for you and your friends to make each other laugh.

In terms of tone, "funny" doesn't necessarily mean "light." Some of our funny games find humor in emotional content. *Hero Dog Saves Town* and *Event Planning in Zero G* are silly and fun, whereas *Unkindness* and *Wonders* find humor in turbulent emotion and interpersonal conflict, which can be heavy for some groups. *Object Kilo* offers a look into the abyss using dry humor. No matter what, these games are most enjoyable when players are excited and able to laugh with them.

Serious: These games work best when players are fully invested. Some RPGs want to take you on an emotional journey and maybe teach you something about yourself. If they are approached earnestly, they can change your life. But if you aren't willing to dive in, they may fall flat.

Games like *Absolution in Brass* and *The Agony of Elves* have premises tied up in fraught emotion and tragedy, which is an acquired taste. *Annedale-by-Sea* and *A Green Hour* are very intimate and can stray out of comfort zones for some players. *What Our Bodies Tell Us* requires players to trust each other enough to draw on each other's skin! More than anything the Serious tag means the game is asking players to approach with care.

Scary: Scary games are either straightforward horror scenarios, or they play with horror tropes. Many RPGs are about empowerment, and horror games often move in the other direction, putting players in situations where their characters are at the mercy of malevolent forces.

Scary games range from simply spooky to tense and gory. *It Wants Souls* and *You Were Never Really Here* are classic ghost stories, while *Dead Planet* is a blood-spattered thriller.

Format

While most games have one GM and several PCs, this collection contains games that accommodate a number of different styles of play. Some players like the GM format, others are happy to move between roles as the game unfolds, and some feel nervous taking on certain responsibilities. The Format tags will tell you the basic format for each game.

Traditional: A Traditional game structure has one GM and one or more PCs. The PCs are in charge of their characters, while the GM controls everything that is not a player character. This is the most popular format for an RPG, and if you are familiar with games like *Dungeons & Dragons*, you understand the basic principle.

Traditional games are great for new players, as they introduce a format that appears in the vast majority of RPGs.

GMless: GMless games move away from the Traditional structure by blurring or removing the line between GM and PC. A GMless game might put every player in a position where they control the world around their characters—it might even do away with the concept of characters entirely. Some GMless games have everyone at the table playing characters and resolve the movement of the rest of the world entirely through game mechanics.

We recommend GMless games for folks who feel confident about playing. They tend to provide less structure and reward players who enthusiastically jump in!

Rotating: Games with a Rotating format have players moving between roles throughout the game. Sometimes players will only be responsible for a single PC; others will have to control the game world and NPCs.

This format is great for players who are interested in experimenting with the GM role but don't feel like they want to hold those responsibilities through the whole game.

Content

Unlike our other tag types Content tags are not connected to larger consistent categories. They are abbreviated descriptors specific to individual games. All of our tags are meant to help you understand what to expect before you commit to a game. Content tags will help you understand things about a game that might not be clear until you start playing.

Now you know what you need to know to play any of the games in this book. Let your imagination run wild and have fun!

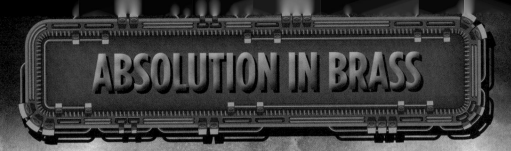

ABSOLUTION IN BRASS

A Game of Guilty Steampunk Zombie-Cyborgs

BY SHARANG BISWAS

Number of players: 3–4 // Playing time: 60–90 minutes
Complexity: 3 // You'll need: Paper and pens.
Goal: Gain forgiveness for your past deeds.
Content Tags: // Genre: Fantasy // Tone: Serious //
Format: Rotating // Content: Emotional, trauma, guilt

In *Absolution in Brass*, you play as a band of steampunk zombie-cyborgs, undead soldiers conscripted by the Wicked Choir, who march toward humanity's last battle while seeking forgiveness for the wrongs they did in the past.

TERMS:

FUSED: Your characters. Brass-undead cyborgs. Your band of Fused knew each other in life and march together in death.

WICKED CHOIR: The enemy of humanity. You are their slaves.

SHARDS OF HEAVEN: Warped geography, where pieces of Heaven landed after the Wicked Choir's decisive attack.

WRONGED: The Fused whose past suffering at the hands of the other Fused is spotlighted at each Shard.

CENSURED: The Fused who hurt the Wronged the most (as chosen by the Wronged). They make a sacrifice at the Shard.

The Wicked Choir's howl shattered Heaven, hurling twisted Shards across the lands.

You died.

Now, you are a "Fused," an undead creature of brass and necrotic flesh.

What dangers have the warped Shards that dot the landscape birthed? Can you overcome the corruption of your decaying body? Will you unearth terrible memories from your life?

And will these memories of guilt, shame, and pain bind you further to the Choir, or will you earn forgiveness and break free from your masters during the Final Battle?

SETUP

All players answer the following questions:

1. What fueled your character's life, or what was the most significant event to happen to your character?

• Beauty • Discovery • Difficult Choices • Labor • People

2. What was your character's occupation in life?

FUEL

The Chorus's other soldiers have been powered by substances such as:

• **BEAUTY:** crushed amber

• **DISCOVERY:** fermented cave-darkness

• **DIFFICULT CHOICES:** the breath of a priest before a sin

• **LABOR:** lightning

• **PEOPLE:** an insect swarm

Answer the following questions:

1. The Choir powers your character's form with a substance that acts as a crude echo of this fuel. What is it?

2. What one possession from life does your character still carry?

3. What physical limitation does your character's brass-undead form impose on you?

4. What is the first initial of your character's name?

You recall little else of your life.

Each player describes their character and how they look.

GAMEPLAY

You march toward the Final Battle. In your way lie Shards of Heaven, which you must traverse.

The Shards are divided into three groups:

- Proximal (nearest to you)
- Medial
- Distal (farthest away)

Your group should begin by choosing a Proximal Shard together. In later rounds, move on to Medial Shards, and finally Distal Shards. You may encounter multiple Distal Shards (see Ending the Game for a full description of these Shards).

AT EACH SHARD

One Fused is "the Wronged." They describe the horrifying landscape and detail the traps or monstrous creatures of the Shard that threaten the band.

Each other Fused answers these questions:

1. What sensory detail described by the Wronged horrifies you?

2. What terrible memory—where you hurt or betrayed the Wronged—is sparked?

3. Did you mean to do it?

The Wronged glimpses these memories. They designate who they feel is the worst offender as "the Censured." The Censured describes how they help the band traverse the Shard and what physical capability they alone sacrifice in the process.

AFTER EVERY SHARD

The band makes camp for as long as it needs to maintain their mechanisms and ease flesh fatigue. Each Fused describes a difficulty they have encountered during the journey due to their physical limitations or sacrifices at the Shards. Each Fused can narrate how they can try to help another Fused with these difficulties, perhaps as a way to atone for their sins.

The last Censured is the new Wronged and decides which Shard the band travels to next.

ENDING THE GAME

After everyone has taken the role of the Wronged once (though you can play longer), the band reaches the Final Battle.

Each Fused:

- Describes one sensory detail about the battle.
- Asks every other Fused, "Do you forgive me?"

Any Fused who have been forgiven by fewer than half the band remain enslaved to the Wicked Choir. They describe their last physical sensation before their will is subsumed.

The other Fused break free. They each describe one joyful memory from their life, which fuels their battle against the Choir.

The game ends right as the Fused join battle. The outcome is not discussed.

PROXIMAL SHARDS

THE MIRROR-DEATH: A reflective fog haunted by silhouettes with torn wings and confusing odors.

THE HALF-SMILE: A forest perpetually aflame, housing a broken sliver of the moon.

THE FOUNTAIN-FERMENT: An enormous wooden fountain caked with rotting cheese, dotted with tiny birds.

MEDIAL SHARDS

THE BEAUTY-THAT-WAS: The petrified body of a colossal woman stretched over a gorge, leaking wine from innumerable cuts.

NEVER-VILLAGE: A collection of paper buildings overrun with childhood-nightmare graffiti.

THE HARDENED GARDEN: An unsettling arrangement of precisely cut geometric slabs of frozen honey.

DISTAL SHARDS

THE SHRILL UNREST: A network of caves plagued by carnivorous colors that chitter relentlessly.

THE FALLEN SCALES: An impossibly complex mechanism shivering with the whispers of unrequited love.

SILENCE: A vast plane of smooth, white marble beset with the ghosts of heretical words.

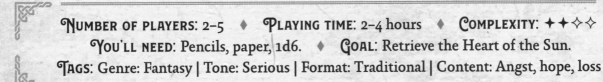

THE Agony OF Elves
A Game about Sadness, Acceptance, and Peril
BY LEVON JIHANIAN

Elves vanished from this land many years ago. They left this cold and changing world to live out their eternal lives in the Twilight Isles. You are elves sent back to the realm of humanity to retrieve the lost Heart of the Sun. You wash ashore on a rocky beach and are suddenly enveloped by unrelenting Grief. Will you find the Heart? Will you accept adversity or succumb to sadness?

NUMBER OF PLAYERS: 2–5 ◆ **PLAYING TIME:** 2–4 hours ◆ **COMPLEXITY:** ✦✦✧✧
YOU'LL NEED: Pencils, paper, 1d6. ◆ **GOAL:** Retrieve the Heart of the Sun.
TAGS: Genre: Fantasy | Tone: Serious | Format: Traditional | Content: Angst, hope, loss

SETUP

One of the players is the Facilitator. Everyone else creates characters to play.

Character Creation

Pick your role and write down the associated stats, shown in the following list. One player must choose the Keeper role:

KEEPER (divide 4 points between strength, reason, and resilience)
LECTOR (strength 0, reason 3, resilience 1)
MAGE (strength 0, reason 2, resilience 2)
PRIESTESS (strength 0, reason 1, resilience 3)
SCOUT (strength 2, reason 2, resilience 0)
SOLDIER (strength 3, reason 0, resilience 1)

The Characters:

1 The **KEEPER** bears the vessel and is tasked with carrying the Heart back to the Twilight Isles.
2 The **LECTOR** is both a source of knowledge and a liaison between the elves and humans.
3 The **MAGE** creates and controls ice and fire.
4 The **PRIESTESS** is the spiritual support for the team. They serve the elf goddess known as the Moon Mother.
5 The **SCOUT** is versed in wayfinding and knows how to protect themselves.
6 The **SOLDIER** knows how to fight. They protect the other characters from harm.

Choose a Downfall by writing down the following options separately and rolling 1 on the d6 for each character. Each player should have a different Downfall:

⚀ **COWARD:** You will cower and hide.
⚁ **DESTROYER:** You will destroy something precious.
⚂ **FOOL:** You will make a grievous error in judgment.
⚃ **HERETIC:** You will renounce the Moon Mother to all who will hear you.
⚄ **IRRESOLUTE:** You will be incapable of making important decisions.
⚅ **TRAITOR:** You will betray the mission for your own benefit.

Choose a Desire or come up with your own. Roll a d6. Characters can share motivations if players are comfortable with the idea, otherwise reroll.

- ⚀ "I must return home to the Twilight Isles as soon as possible."
- ⚁ "I must prove myself to the Moon Mother."
- ⚂ "I must win the heart of my fellow journey elf."
- ⚃ "I must show everyone I am the best among us."
- ⚄ "I must never leave this beautiful and nightmarish land."
- ⚅ "I must bring order to the clumsy and brutal humans."

Name your character and assign to them a special unique item. Make sure each character has a different item:

1 A gilded sword that shows your high station
2 A secret decree from the elven high chancellor
3 A hairbrush given to you by the Moon Mother herself
4 A rare magical cloak of disguise
5 An enchanted silk glove
6 An owl companion

⚘ GAMEPLAY ⚘

The elves start on the rocky shore and disembark from their small boat. It is night, and their shadows dance among the cliff walls as they sit around the campfire. The ocean roars.

The game goes through five scenes. The Facilitator decides when to end a scene and move on.

1 The Rocky Shore
2 The Human Village
3 The Thieves' Road
4 The Gray Forest
5 The Sun King's Crypt
6 The Sun King's Wrath

At the beginning of the first scene, each player introduces their character, and reveals their Desire. The elves then move on to scene 2: The Human Village.

At the beginning of each subsequent scene, the Facilitator rolls a d6 to determine the Trouble of the scene.

- ⚀ Mist of Desolation
- ⚁ Human Fools
- ⚂ The Night Beast
- ⚃ Ghosts of the Broken
- ⚄ The Thing in the Mirror
- ⚅ The Specter of Grief

Actions and Tests

When a character faces a task where the outcome is in question, or when the Facilitator asks them to test a stat, they roll a die and add the most appropriate stat to the roll. If the result is 6 or more, the character succeeds.

On a 5 or less, the Facilitator changes or adds something to the player's character sheet. This could be:

- ♦ **A change to a stat**
- ♦ **A fact** (e.g., "you broke leg" or "the grace of the Moon Mother no longer glows upon you")
- ♦ **A feeling or perception** (e.g., "you feel you have been lied to" or "there's something about the humans that you find alluring")
- ♦ **The removal of an item from your possession**

Whether the action succeeds or fails is then up to the Facilitator. If the player doesn't like what the Facilitator has changed, they can cancel the change by marking down a Grief point.

Grief

Elves have indefinite life spans and don't age once they reach adulthood. While all humans succumb to mortality, all elves ultimately succumb to Grief. Characters accrue Grief when canceling a failed check. The Facilitator can also ask for a resilience test in certain circumstances. If the test fails, the player accrues Grief.

Once 3 points of Grief are inflicted, the elf is Broken and must play out their assigned Downfall. A Broken elf loses their grace and immortality and can never return to the Twilight Isles.

⚘ ENDING THE GAME ⚘

The game is over when the elves recover the Heart of the Sun, or when they all die or succumb to Grief.

Annedale-by-Sea

An Epistolary Game
by Jay Dragon

The small town of Annedale-by-Sea is about a day trip away from the Big City. Two people play asynchronously over the course of multiple weeks or months by writing letters to each other.

Number of players: 2 • Playing time: As long as you both want to keep playing • Complexity: ■ ■ ■ □ • You'll need: Paper, pens, standard deck of playing cards with jokers removed. • Goal: To develop an interesting and complex correspondence. • Tags: Genre–Modern, Tone–Serious, Format–GMless, Content–Romance, emotional, transgender

SETUP

In this game, there are two possible characters:

Marnie grew up in the town of Annedale-by-Sea. They went to college but dropped out quickly and remains in Annedale. Two of the following words are always true about Marnie, and one of them is always false. The player who plays Marnie chooses which words are true and which is false.

↳ Honest, Cheerful, Naive, Weary, Caring, Lonely

Ridley also grew up in the town of Annedale-by-Sea but left for the Big City a couple of weeks ago. They promised to stay in touch with their friend Marnie. Two of the following words are always true about Ridley, and one of them is always false. The player who plays Ridley chooses which words are true and which is false.

↳ Passionate, Funny, Emotional, Mature, Thoughtful, Socialite

Establish topics you feel comfortable with or interested in writing about and topics that you'd like to avoid. Here is a list of topics you cannot write about:

- The Ongoing War
- Marnie's parents
- Ridley's deadname
- That time on the beach in the darkness, with just the two of you, and what happened that night

Together, choose one topic to remove from this list, and add anything else you'd like to forbid due to narrative dramatics or practical safety. Finally, ask each other three questions.

Marnie, ask Ridley:

- What was your favorite part about the long seaside walks we used to go on?
- Why don't I feel okay leaving Annedale?
- How is my relationship with Oma, whom I live with?

Ridley, ask Marnie:

- What happened in the hotel room on our trip to the Big City?
- What made Annedale feel like it wasn't my home anymore?
- What is my tiny apartment in the Big City like?

GAMEPLAY

Something went down at work today. What was it? Choose from the table or create your own. Roll the d6 and choose one of the following:

1. **Natural disaster**
2. **Supernatural occurrence**
3. **Melodramatic confession**
4. **Heated confrontation**
5. **Unexpected appearance of an animal**
6. **Choose your own**

You all have different angles on the story—but now is your chance to prove that your version of whatever happened is worthy of you being sent home early. Do whatever it takes to convince your coworkers that you deserve to be sent home. The trick here is to convince them you are worthy while simultaneously convincing them that you haven't stepped all over them to get there.

The first Employee declares which action to use as a lens for their story (Rant, Gush, Dish, or Throwdown) and begins to explain what happened. They have 60 seconds to explain themselves as clearly as possible.

- **RANT:** Complain about something a coworker/manager/guest did that made your job harder. Make sure everyone knows how unfair, rude, inconsiderate, and wrong it is.
- **GUSH:** Describe an amazing, magical, breathtaking moment that has happened between you and a guest/manager/coworker. Will it lead to promotion, a positive mark on your record...or even romance?
- **DISH:** Let everyone at the table in on some fresh, hot gossip. Start a rumor, share a scandal, repeat what you overheard, or describe how a coworker got in trouble while you were watching.
- **THROWDOWN:** Someone at the table did something that either affects you directly or threatens your best friend (whom you would die for). It forces you to call them out on their sh*t. Right now. This is a drastic move that allows the object of your Throwdown to have an equal amount of time to respond to the accusation. Everyone witnessing then votes on who "won" the Throwdown. The loser is ineligible to receive votes for that round.

When the 60 seconds is up, the next Employee has 60 seconds and their choice of action to tell the story. If someone appears to be swaying the story against you, find a way to pitch them in an even worse light when it's your turn.

After the first round, everyone votes for who they think deserves to go home by writing down the color of their shirt (or the player's name) on a scrap of paper. You cannot vote for yourself. Fold up the paper and place it in the hat or container.

Play another round with 30 seconds per player. Vote again.

The third round has only 15 seconds. Vote again.

The final round has 5 seconds. This is your last chance! Pull out all the stops. Give your most *desperate* excuse as to why you should go home early—even if it's seemingly unrelated to the story! Vote again.

ENDING THE GAME

The time has come! As a group, unfold all the papers and count how many votes each Employee got. The Employee with the most votes wins and is presented to Manager Greg for early release. The winner says a snarky one-liner before they clock out for the day.

ALTERNATE ENDING

The winner flips a coin: If it's heads, Greg lets them go home; tails, he keeps them on the clock, and the coin passes to the Employee with the second-most votes. Depending on the coin flip, someone with very few votes might go home instead...or maybe *nobody goes home early*. Brutal, but that's work for you. Adulting is hard.

BREAKING RANK

A Role-Playing Fantasy of Rebellion and Reflection

BY NELL RABAN

SETUP

One person should facilitate the game; the Facilitator should read ahead and familiarize themselves with the rules and adventure. Everyone else should create their own characters, using the following steps.

CREATING CHARACTERS

Each character should have a career, skills, gifts, and a wish. Players should also give their character a name, pronouns, and an appearance.

1. Choose a former career and three skills.

(For one- or two-character parties, choose a fourth skill from another career.) Your character was trained so they could serve.

Agent: disguises, dodging, infiltration, misdirection, underworld

Artificer: alchemy, logic, mechanics, medicine, science

Envoy: bureaucracy, convincing, history, leadership, negotiation

Sentinel: awareness, defense, fighting, tactics, threatening

2. Choose or create three gifts and describe who gave them to you.

Gifts make life worth living.

Examples: ancestral weapon, coin purse, cookbook, enchanted cloak, glowing jewel, language, lockpick set, map, penknife, rare concoction, shield, spell, spyglass, toolkit, watch

3. Make a wish.

What does your character want out of life, going forward?

Number of players: 2–5

Playing time: 2–4 hours

Complexity: ● ● ○ ○

You'll need: 4d6 per person, notepaper, writing utensils.

Goal: Destroy your dossiers and escape the Hall of Records.

Tags: Genre: Science Fiction; Tone: Adventurous; Format: Traditional; Content: Suspense, stealth, guilt

TOP SECRET

GAMEPLAY

The Facilitator starts the game by reading this aloud:

You were all loyal to Summrial once, before you saw the truth of its evil ways. You've chosen to defect, taking with you the skills you learned and the gifts that you cherish. There's only one thing left to do before you can start your life over: Go to the Hall of Records and destroy your own dossier, which contains everything the Summrial Dominion knows of you and your service.

It wasn't easy, but you're in. There's a stillness in this empty corridor, but there are more obstacles ahead. Learn the location of the dossiers and make your way there so that you can do what must be done.

At this point, open the game up to the players. Have them solve problems related to learning the dossiers' location and getting there.

If things seem to go too smoothly for the players, throw them one or two more problems, such as:

- Locked doors
- Sentries
- Clerks
- Traps
- Distractions
- Puzzles

In order to resolve these problems, players can take Actions. When a player takes an Action, they roll 2d6. A 6 is a success. The Facilitator will say how many successes are needed for the Action, according to its difficulty. If players possess skills that are applicable to resolving the problem, they may roll an additional die for each applicable skill.

Players may increase the range of possible successes by 1 (from just 6 to 5–6, for example) for each applicable gift, down to 4–6.

Note that no skill or gift grants an automatic success.

GROUP ACTIONS

Players are encouraged to work together, especially in difficult situations, by adding their skills and gifts to one base roll. Each should narrate how they contribute to the overall effort.

Some things that will improve your gameplay include:

- Personalize the problems to the characters
- Draw maps
- Encourage quick, simple ideas over laborious plans
- Increase difficulty over time

Once the characters have the dossiers in hand, the Facilitator will read this text aloud:

You take a moment to read your own files. You recognize some of it—your time in training, your achievements, the life you lived in between. You wonder what's worth keeping, and what's best forgotten. Are the skills you now possess, though useful, worth the evil they served? Are the gifts, though a comfort, enough to aid you in the days ahead? You don't have room in your heart for both.

If you choose your skills, permanently increase the success range to 5–6 and cross off your gifts.

If you choose your gifts, roll 3 dice from now on and cross off your skills.

The characters can't just escape the same way they came in. The Facilitator rolls a d6 and determines if:

⚀ They lost their sense of direction

⚁ A clerk wanders into the room

⚂ They've tripped an alarm and are forced to scatter

⚃ They're captured

⚄ One character has been separated from the party and must be found

⚅ Someone has locked the door from the outside

Give them one or two more problems on their way out. Once they escape the Hall of Records and are a safe distance away, the Facilitator reads this aloud:

And that's it. You're free. There's no longer a record you ever existed. Now what?

ENDING THE GAME

Breaking Rank is over when the player characters have destroyed their own dossiers and escaped the Hall of Records.

BROKEN SWORDS and TWISTED TRAILS

A Game of Marching Bravely Into the Dungeon ...and Maybe Crawling Out

By BRANDON LEON-GAMBETTA

NUMBER OF PLAYERS: 2–6: 1 Dungeon Master (DM), the rest Heroes

PLAYING TIME: 1–2 hours

COMPLEXITY: ♦♦♦◇

YOU'LL NEED: 2d6 (ideally 1 per player), pens or pencils, 6 notecards per player.

GOAL: Fight an enormous threat to your home and maybe even survive.

TAGS:
Genre: Fantasy
Tone: Adventurous
Format: Traditional
Content: Classic, player-driven creativity

You will be playing Heroes of a kingdom preparing to battle against the monsters who threaten your home. Play consists of a brief character creation segment followed by three encounters in which your Heroes will face challenges to save their home.

SETUP

Give each player six notecards. On five of their notecards players should write Traits (one Trait per card): abilities, magics, treasures, and other character features. Each player keeps one notecard and puts the rest into a Treasure pile. Once the Treasure pile is created and shuffled, players draw a second Trait.

Based on their two Traits, players should choose a name and pronouns for their character, write them on the final notecard, and fold the card into a nameplate that everyone can read. Going around the table, players should introduce their characters in a few sentences.

Monster Creation

Roll 1d6 on the following tables to create the threat to the kingdom or make your own:

⚀	An enormous	Dragon	Who wishes to eat everyone
⚁	An honorable	Demon	Seeking political power
⚂	A mastermind	Vampire	Creating a dark ritual
⚃	A romantic	Automaton	Who wishes only to kill
⚄	A sneaky	Wizard	With a massive army
⚅	An undead	Warlord	Amassing a fortune

Talk through your threat as a group and detail it. Be sure to give it a name, a motivation, pronouns, and immense power.

GAMEPLAY

The DM's job is to describe situations and threats, make challenges feel dangerous, and ask lots of questions. The Heroes' job is to drive forward, tell stories, and win or die gracefully.

The DM begins by describing what the first dangerous stop on the journey is like. Be sure to describe how things look, sound, and smell, as well as any feelings the Heroes get. The Challenge Rating of a Dungeon is the amount of successes the players will need to roll combined in order to defeat and escape the dungeon. Challenge Rating is determined by number of players and which of the three Dungeons they are in.

Challenge Ratings

DUNGEON 1: Players +1
DUNGEON 2: Players +2
FINAL DUNGEON: Players +3

The DM will tell the players about a threatening situation in this location that the Heroes will have to deal with in order to pass. Heroes take turns clockwise from the DM describing how they deal with the threat and whether they are Acting <u>Heroically</u> (like a brave hero in a story) or Acting <u>Desperately</u> (just trying to scrape by alive).

By default, Traits are Unscarred, representing gear or abilities working well or in good repair. When these Traits become Scarred, the player flips the card and writes a damaged, corrupted, or desperate version on the other side. The DM determines...

♦ If they Act <u>Heroically</u>, they roll 2d6+ their Unscarred Traits.
♦ If they Act <u>Desperately</u>, they roll 2d6+ their Scarred Traits.

On a 10+, for either roll, they succeed decisively, describe their success, and the DM lowers the Challenge Rating by 1.

On a 7–9, they succeed at a cost and describe their success, but they or the DM will complicate it. The Challenge Rating lowers by 1, *but*:

♦ If they Acted <u>Heroically</u>, they Scar a Trait.
♦ If they Acted <u>Desperately</u>, they take an Injury and draw a Skull on their nameplate.

On a 6-, the threat pushes forward on them. The DM will Scar a Trait or give them an Injury (DM's choice), and the Challenge Rating doesn't drop.

No Hero can roll twice in a row, and all Heroes must act before a Hero can act again. If the current threat is dealt with fully before the Challenge Rating hits 0, the DM may describe additional threats within the same location.

When the Challenge hits 0, the last Hero to roll describes how the party escapes the Dungeon, and all players draw a Treasure, the discarded traits from the beginning.

Between Dungeons, the players travel, and each one says what wonders they see on the road. Then they enter the Dungeon again.

ENDING THE GAME

Once you have cleared two Dungeons, you come to the final lair. The DM and the players should work together to describe the lair of the Great Threat.

From there, play continues as normal for a Dungeon, with one exception: If a player rolls their number of Injuries or lower (marked by the Skulls drawn on their nameplate), they die.

When a Hero dies <u>Heroically</u>, give the player a chance to describe their glorious fighting. They aren't slain because they were weak or cowardly but because their bravery is so great! Additionally, they may choose to rally their friends (giving a +1 to an ally's next roll) or make a final desperate strike lowering the Challenge Rating by 1.

When a Hero dies <u>Desperately</u>, give the player a chance to describe their glorious fighting. They aren't slain because they were weak or cowardly but because their opposition was too powerful! Additionally, they may choose to rally their friends (giving a +1 to an ally's next roll) or make a final desperate strike lowering the Challenge Rating by 1.

When the Challenge Rating hits 0, the Great Threat is defeated.

All Heroes who live tell a story of their life after. All Heroes who fell tell a story of how they are remembered.

BY ASH McALLAN

DEAD PLANET
MARTIAN RECON TEAM ALPHA

NUMBER OF PLAYERS: 3–5 **PLAYING TIME:** 2–4 hours
COMPLEXITY: ● ● ● ● **YOU'LL NEED:** Paper, pens, at least 5 d6s per player, 1 straw per player with 1 cut shorter than the others. **GOAL:** Discover the cause of the destruction of the Mars colony. **TAGS:** Genre: Science Fiction | Tone: Scary | Format: Rotating | Content: Gore, body horror, tragic horror

Four months ago, after a century of settlement, Mars stopped responding to all Earth communications. Your crew has been sent to investigate.

SETUP

Each character assigns 7 points among the following 12 actions with no more than 2 in any one action.

- ● MECHANICAL CONSTRUCTION
- ● PROGRAMMING
- ● CHEMISTRY
- ● BOTANY
- ● MEDICINE
- ● COMBAT
- ● DANCE
- ● ATHLETICS
- ● PERSUASION
- ● COUNSELING
- ● OBSERVATION
- ● INVESTIGATION

Each player takes a turn doing the following: Describe your character's appearance and explain why they were sent on this mission. Choose a name and pronouns. Now, choose another player and decide with them why you loathe them. This hatred does not have to be reciprocal, but it can be.

Choose another player and decide with them why you love them. This does not have to be reciprocal, but it can be. Continue until each player has completed all actions.

clocks

Clocks are a way to track progress toward or away from outcomes. A clock is a circle divided into segments by bisecting lines. When it moves, segments are filled in or erased. A clock might show progress toward the construction of an air filter or healing a wound.

○ AIR FILTER COMPLETE

ONE MIGHT SHOW THE DEPLETION OF RATIONS, STARTING FULL AND EMPTYING OVER TIME

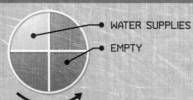

○ WATER SUPPLIES

WATER SUPPLIES
EMPTY

ANOTHER MIGHT START HALFWAY FULL TO INDICATE COMPETING FORCES, WITH OUTCOMES AT BOTH ENDS

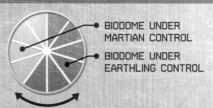

○ BIODOME

BIODOME UNDER MARTIAN CONTROL
BIODOME UNDER EARTHLING CONTROL

GAMEPLAY

As your ship approaches Mars and begins its descent, you see smoke from the massive colony structures. As the ship shakes, passing through the atmosphere, there is a loud *zap!* and the lights die.

Each player draws a straw.

Take turns discussing what to do as you hurtle toward the Martian surface in the dark. If a player says, "We're going to

die," the ship crashes. (If no one says this, continue this segment of the game until one of the characters says, "We're going to die!") Make sounds as appropriate.

The player who drew the short straw dies in the crash (however, the player running this now-dead character continues to have a role in the game).

you're Alive

Once you have crash-landed on the Dead Planet, your intention is to survive. The ship is wrecked and so, too, is the colony. There are no means to communicate with Earth. Supplies are low. Explore, investigate, repair what you can, and try to get home.

Whenever you try to do something tricky like rescuing a power cell from unstable wreckage, or severing a limb pinned in a malfunctioning gate, you should roll an Action.

Action Rolls

When you roll an Action, you must establish your approach and intent and what you are trying to achieve. Whoever is playing the dead character will tell you which Action it sounds like you are using and whether Success would complete your goal or advance a clock. If you disagree, they can change their intent and/or approach.

The player who rolls the Action should take the number of d6s equal to the points they have in the Action being used.

For each additional factor in your favor (as determined by the dead person), take an extra die. For each additional factor against you, drop one die. Roll the dice you have and take the highest result. If you have no dice, instead roll 2d and take the lowest result.

On a 1–3: Failure and consequences

On a 4–5: Success or move 1 clock segment, but with consequences

On a 6: Success or move 2 clock segments

On multiple 6s: Great Success or move 4 clock segments

If multiple characters work together like combining efforts to push and free the wheels of a rover, they all roll, and the highest result is used. For each result 1–3, the character leading the Action takes 1 Stress.

When something bad happens, including consequences, you may resist it.

Explain how you avoid, negate, or lessen its impact and roll the appropriate Action.

On a 1–3: You do not resist it; it happens

On a 4–5: You resist it but take 2 Stress

On a 6: You successfully resist it

When you attempt to construct or repair things (fix machines, heal bones, grow food), you must explain to the dead character what each thing does. The dead character will explain what you will need, how long it will take, and what flaws, if any, it has. Then start a clock to track progress toward completion and use actions to progress it.

stress

When characters take Stress, they fill in segments on an 8-segment clock. When the clock is full, the player empties it and chooses which one of the following symptoms the character develops:

1. PARANOIA
2. PANIC AND DESPAIR
3. HYPERAGGRESSION
4. DELUSIONS
5. APATHY AND FATIGUE
6. RISK-TAKING BEHAVIOR

If a character's Stress clock fills a second time, the character leaves the party and falls under the collective control of the dead player, whom the character's player joins.

Spending an hour sleeping, relaxing, or socializing clears 1 Stress.

Dead

Welcome to the Dead Planet. You are not going home.

When your character is dead, it is your responsibility to collectively, with any other dead players, describe Mars. As the living explore Mars, the dead collectively describe the ruins of the colony and whatever else they encounter within or without.

When a live player rolls less than 6 on an Action, the dead must impose consequences from this list:

1. SOMEONE IS INJURED OR KILLED
2. SOMEONE TAKES STRESS
3. THE PARTY'S SUCCESS IS LIMITED
4. EQUIPMENT OR RESOURCES ARE LOST
5. A CLOCK MOVES
6. THE SITUATION WORSENS

ENDING THE GAME

Through their shared narration the dead players should fill the planet with terror, honor the living, and play to find out what happens. Note that the dead cannot take any physical actions.

DISTANT STARS

A GAME ABOUT MAKING MISTAKES

BY LAURA SIMPSON

NUMBER OF PLAYERS: 4

PLAYING TIME: Approximately 90 minutes

COMPLEXITY: ★ ★ ★ ☆

YOU'LL NEED: Paper, pencils.

GOAL: To discover the real reasons we are alone in the universe.

TAGS:

Genre: Science Fiction

Tone: Serious

Format: Rotating

Content: Failure, guilt, regret

Each player in *Distant Stars* represents a team member who has returned from a failed First Contact mission. This mission lasted six months and was going to be a turning point for human civilization. The failure was devastating and set back interstellar knowledge and travel by a century. Each team member made a poor decision, a mistake that led to the failure of the mission. The players are now giving statements to an official inquiry into the mission's failure.

SETUP

1. Read this game text aloud or give each player the opportunity to do so silently.
2. Decide who will play which character. The characters are listed on the following page.
3. Decide what the First Briefing looks like. In character, players play through the First Briefing to establish their characters' interaction. Each player should select the scene they will take responsibility for.
4. Create a blank timeline of the mission, from arrival to failure.
5. Play the four scenes.
6. Reconcile.

GAMEPLAY

The game is composed of four scenes that take place in the format of a congressional hearing. Add each scene and flashback to the timeline after completing them.

One character is the focus of each scene. The scenes are:

Mistake 1: We underestimated what they had and overestimated what we could offer.

How did we overestimate our role?

Mistake 2: We spoke more than we listened.

How did we misunderstand the extraterrestrials?

Mistake 3: We were untrustworthy.

What seemed like a great idea that backfired?

Mistake 4: We were aggressive.

When did we realize that we went too far?

SCENES

During your character's scene, you have three responsibilities: to frame the scene, set up a flashback to show where you made a critical mistake, and to end the scene.

TO FRAME THE SCENE

- Start with an introduction to the lead team member. The character describes who they are and their role on the team. Give an "official" description of the encounter with the alien civilization, who else was there, and what your character did in relation to the other characters.
- Begin the scene with the idea of portraying your character in a positive light. Your character definitely messed up, but don't lie outright.

GOALS

During your scene, your goal is to tell the official story and the truth of the mistake made.

That goal is accomplished by:

- Framing the scene (who, what, where, and when)
- Adding the event that occurs in the scene to the timeline
- Deciding who will be in the scene and assigning any supporting characters (for instance, the aliens with whom you made contact)
- Playing through the scene (note that during this first playthrough, the character who is testifying is spinning it to put the least amount of blame on themselves)
- Stopping at the place of the mistake
- Retelling the scene via flashback, now revealing the truth of what happened; this truth can come from the other participants in the scene, which occurs in the form of a Reveal of the Truth
- Ending the scene with the "official ending"
- You can use monologues to express hidden desire, and Reveals of Truth to express past failure and the truth of the situation

REVEAL OF TRUTH

To start the Reveal of Truth, your character will choose a point in the scene to show where they made the critical mistake on the mission. They then insert a mini-scene around when they make this error. The mini-scene is added to the timeline. To initiate the mini-scene, the focus character will point at themselves and state: "This is where I made a mistake."

This scene may include some of the Astronauts or characters assigned to other players. The lead player assigns these roles and describes the scene in first person.

Play out the Reveal of Truth until the focus character feels the mistake was clear. End the flashback by saying, "Cut." Reenter the scene by saying, "I regret that."

ENDING THE SCENE

The scene ends when the focus character feels like they have covered both the "official story" and the truth of their mistake. End the scene by saying, "That was the event to my best recollection." Each scene should last about 15 minutes.

MONOLOGUES

At any time, a player may point to themselves or another and say, "Monologue." The monologue should be a brief statement, where the player reveals their character's hidden desires or fear. Other players may use the revealed information to play toward or against the character's desires. After monologuing, play resumes.

ENDING THE GAME

After the final scene has ended, each character gives an epilogue: a few short sentences framing the future for this character after the hearing.

RECONCILE

Sit in a circle with your coplayers to wrap up your characters' storylines.

While still in character, address the other three characters by name, and state how your character could have helped them.

After each player has completed their resolutions, set aside your characters and discuss a moment from the game that you enjoyed. Address each player by their actual name.

CAST

Amina: Diplomat

- Status: 5. (Status aids role-playing by telling the players how senior their character is to other members of the group.)
- Demeanor: Arrogant, quick.
- Tension: You're damn sure that Brent deliberately delivers your briefings late.

Brent: Xeno Linguist

- Status: 2.
- Demeanor: Burned-out, overextended.
- Tension: Carla is a spy. She definitely went through your office.

Jelani: Xeno Anthropologist

- Status: 2.
- Demeanor: Disempowered, checked out.
- Tension: Amina is the worst and best part of the mission, and she won't let you forget it.

Carla: Captain

- Status: 4.
- Demeanor: Secretive, aggressive.
- Tension: Jelani is silent on all the matters that are important, and the reverse for everything else.

DOOMED STARS

LOVE, DESTRUCTION, and ★ CHANGE in the STARS ★

By ADIRA SLATTERY

You are two stars in a binary star system, and you are in love.
But this love is bittersweet, as you have been so far apart.
Always dancing around the other in the heavens, never touching.
But recently, something has happened.
You have each begun to move toward the other star!

NUMBER OF PLAYERS 2

PLAYING TIME 1–2 hours

COMPLEXITY ★★★

YOU'LL NEED
2 sheets of paper, assorted markers and pens.

GOAL
Experience the explosive emotions of two stars who love each other to their mutual destruction.

TAGS
Genre: *Science Fiction*
Tone: *Serious*
Format: *GMless*
Content: *Romance, over-the-top drama*

While you both know that drifting toward the other star spells your eventual demises, you can't help but be a little elated and excited. Something new will be created in your destruction, something created from your love.

SETUP

Clear off a table or find a wide flat area to play on. Consider a bed, a couch, or the floor.

Discuss consent and any boundaries beforehand, as this game includes romance. Reference the safety tools described in the introduction to this book.

Star Creation

★ **Choose your Lifecycle:** *proto, main, subgiant, giant, supergiant, hypergiant, dwarf, subdwarf*

★ **Choose your Appearance:** *black, blue, bright, brown, neutron, red, white, yellow*

★ **Choose your Disposition:** *bold, brooding, cheerful, curious, energetic, nervous, patient, shy*

Once you have chosen your options, begin drawing your star on one of the pages in a way that represents all its qualities. Keep your drawing to one side of the paper, and do your best to communicate your choices. Avoid writing any words; just use pictures.

After you finish drawing, the two of you collaborate in naming your star system. Possibly Antares, Aquarii, Centauri, Lyrae, Persei, Rigel, Sirius, or Spica. One of you is the A star, and one of you is the B star. It does not matter, and you do not know, which is which. Only humans care about such distinctions. You are stars.

GAMEPLAY

Place your drawings on opposite ends of the play area with both hands along the sides of the page so you can easily slide it forward. When you are ready, look at the other player and make as much eye contact as possible. Take a moment of silence as the universe stretches around you. You are stars, and there is nothing else quite like the other in this space. Contemplate your drawings as you breathe.

After time has passed, one player begins by speaking. Choose one of the following options, and elaborate freely for the next few minutes.

- Tell a story about the other star, sharing a memory of a time they did something that intrigued or attracted your star. Expose your star's inner monologue.
- Tell a story about a time your star tried to communicate with the other star. What did they try to say? How did it come across?
- Describe something about the other star that your star has just now noticed as they've moved closer. This discovery should be something your star admires.
- Describe one of the things that orbits around both of you. Is it a planet? A comet? A starship? Or something else entirely? How does it make you feel?
- Explain an event that happened out in the space surrounding you. Did new life arise on a planet? Did two planets crash into each other? Was a faraway star born? Did it die? How did the event make you feel?

When the first player has finished, the other player responds by saying, "And we pull ever closer" and then slides their paper two to four inches toward the first player's. The first player should avoid sliding their page back.

Then switch roles, each player choosing one of the options. Continue back and forth, each affirming their inevitable crash as they slide their stars forward. Whenever possible, build on the stories you both tell and incorporate the events and objects the other player introduces into the narrative. Together, create a complete solar system during the course of the game.

ENDING THE GAME

Once your stars are touching, they collide. The stars are pushed together and embrace tightly like lovers or old friends. Crumple your papers together, intermingling your drawings. Then, you erupt and explode together. Celebrate this light and warmth through high fives, fist pumps, and dancing. Make noises as your explosion lights up the universe.

After you have both exploded, do the following together in a conversation. Build on each other's ideas.

- Describe what is left after the stellar collision. Do you collapse into one star? Do you create a nebula? Do you leave a black hole?
- Spread the pages out flat onto the play area, star-side down. Place the two blank sides of each piece of paper together where you first collided and then draw this new creation. Each of you should contribute to the drawing.

Event Planning
IN ZERO G

EVERYTHING IS FINE • BY JENN MARTIN

NUMBER OF PLAYERS 2–8
PLAYING TIME 2–4 HOURS
COMPLEXITY ✦ ✦ ✦ ✦
YOU'LL NEED 1 OR MORE D6.
GOAL TO PLAN THE GREATEST PARTY IN THE GALAXY.

TAGS:
GENRE SCIENCE FICTION
TONE FUNNY
FORMAT GMLESS
CONTENT WHIMSICAL, FARCICAL, WEIRD ALIEN STUFF

Some of the galaxy's best event planners have gathered to plan the celebration for the Gantrofax's final molting. What an honor to be chosen for this! Of course, we have limited time and an even more limited budget. We couldn't actually afford the galaxy's best, though, so some are…fine. Everything is fine. Happy molting!

Setup

One person should play the Party Planner. Others are Specialists; decide what your specialty is.

FOOD: A delicacy to one species is an insult to another, and you are a master at finding just the right dish for every species for every occasion. Yum!

ATMOSPHERE: Some aliens breathe different gases, and some don't breathe at all. All of the guests need to survive the party, and you've got the skills to make that happen—with color-changing fog, even.

MUSIC/SOUND: Beings without ears can still experience sound, and you know just the right

tones to use, whether it's vibrating bass or gentle nails on a chalkboard.

DECOR: Colors are stimulating, and you speak that language fluently. Whether it's a splash of mauve lighting or a fluorescent black floor, you've got the knack.

GUEST LIST: When one species is food to another, the seating chart gets…complicated. But you've got it all under control, managing curious customs and watching out for who is toxic to whom.

ENTERTAINMENT: You've got a giant space address file; you know performers from all over the galaxy and, critically, what it takes to get them here.

GRAVITY: Gravity is a sensitive topic—everyone wants it perfect, but nobody wants to talk about it. You know what feels just right to all the guests.

PARTY PLANNER (GAME FACILITATOR): The elusive being who ties it all together! You keep the wheels turning and make sure food is served, guests are entertained, and the host is happy.

Any player can introduce new species of aliens, add details to the established universe, or remove elements from the game that make them uncomfortable at any time. Consider removing the human species at the start of the game!

Gameplay

Specialists pitch their plans. Bring your most lavish and decadent ideas and describe them in detail. They will almost certainly be cut for budgetary reasons, but you never know. At the end of the pitch, roll 1d6 and tell the Party Planner what you got; this is your Plan roll.

During each pitch, the Party Planner assigns a number from 1–6 to that pitch. If the Specialist rolled that number on their die, they get the budget for Plan A! If they were off by 1–2, they can do most of their pitch but in a simpler or less expensive way—let's call it Plan B. If they were within 3–4, they can do a decent version of Plan C. If they were 5 away, they are left with Plan Z, the thing they didn't plan or prep for, but maybe it'll turn out great! (Note: If several players roll the number for Plan A, they all get to do the plan they wanted.)

If you don't have a Party Planner, all Specialists proceed with Plan Z.

PREP

The Party Planner sets the scene, describing how perfect everything will be. Once all plans are sorted out, the Party Planner will walk the group through the plan: how guests will experience this party through space and time, culminating with the Gantrofax's final molting. Specialists are encouraged to ask questions here!

Specialists roll 1d6 to determine how well they're able to execute their vision: 6 being perfect, and 1 being a disaster. This is their Prep roll. The Party Planner makes a note of what everyone rolled, paying attention to any matching numbers rolled.

If you don't have a Party Planner, act as if everyone rolled the same number; this will not end well. If there are doubles, you add a problem to the party for every instance of doubles. If everyone rolls doubles, then the party is a total failure.

PARTY!

Specialists each narrate a short scene of a guest enjoying their experience. If none of the Specialists rolled the same number, the party goes off without any conflict! What a happy molting, indeed! Specialists narrate how their expertise was enjoyed or appreciated by guests.

Ending the Game

If Specialists did roll the same numbers in their Prep rolls, drama happens! Specialists detail how their plan went off script—from funny faux pas to bloodshed. Repeat for each set of doubles/triples/etc. Narrate how a guest's experience was confusing or disappointing.

If every Specialist rolled the same number or there was no Party Planner, the party is a massive failure! Specialists narrate how their plan missed the mark entirely or failed in spectacular fashion.

That's a wrap, folks! Enjoy that after-party glow, unless you're in jail.

A Hero Is a Hero, No Matter How Small
Gnomesteaders
By Drew Mierzejewski

You are a seven-inch-tall Gnomish Hero, called by your fellow gnomes to lead them from tragedy to a new land of promise. Only you and your compatriot heroic gnomes can create hope from loss in a world that towers over you.

Number of players: 2–5

Playing time: 2–3 hours

Complexity: ● ● ○

You'll need: 1d6; scrap paper for writing down character names and Occupations and for keeping track of Stress; pens or pencils.

Goal: To successfully settle a new land and help your people survive.

Tags:
Genre: Fantasy
Tone: Adventurous
Format: GMless
Content: Hope, community building, survival

SETUP

Each player creates a character using this character creation section. Once you have created a character, announce them to the group with their name, Occupation, season, and brief physical description. The first player will indicate the next person to announce a character. Do this until all characters are created.

Character and Occupation Creation

Give your character a name. Examples: Lief, Frida, Knud, Helga, Skarde, Sigrid, Svend, Yrsa, Odger, Ulfhild.

Choose an Occupation from the following list. Once another player has chosen an Occupation, you cannot choose it.

The Warrior: Once a chapter you may add +1 to any roll that involves attacking, defending, or martial strategy.

The Rover: Once a chapter you may add +1 to any roll that involves sneaking, hunting, or gathering.

The Crafter: Once a chapter you may add +1 to any roll that involves crafting things, planning, or building.

The Sage: Once a chapter you may add +1 to any roll that involves gathering knowledge, implementing plans, or knowing information.

The Oracle: Once a chapter you may add +1 to any roll that involves superstition, rituals/ceremonies, or magic.

The Trickster: Once a chapter you may add +1 to any roll that involves deception, trickery, or spying.

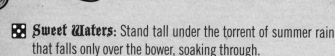

⚁ Sweet Waters: Stand tall under the torrent of summer rain that falls only over the bower, soaking through.

⚄ Root Crown: Roots erupt from the leaf litter, shining bone-white, and wind around you and your betrothed.

GAMEPLAY

There are **Three Parts** to *A Green Hour*.

1. Part One is **Alone Together**.
   Your last conversation as humans, before your union and transformation.
2. Part Two of the game is **A New God**.
   Your wedding altar is the loom on which you weave together your ritual mantles, to create a single, powerful new land god.
3. Part Three ends the game with **The Path Before You**, which takes place one hundred years from the events of A New God. Did you return to the temple and assume your sworn duties to the land? Or did you run?

At the end of each part, you will each roll both 2d6 twice. For the first roll, add the higher result to your Honorable stat. For the second roll, add the higher result to your Impious stat.

If your score exceeds 8 for Honorable, you are granted a boon, and something unexpected and beautiful will spring forth as the child of your union, and the land will heal. Together, describe your boon, the aspects of both of you that it embodies, and how it is essential to the new way of things.

If your score exceeds 8 for Impious, you have the option to deny your fate. To do so will free you, and you both will remain human, but your freedom will doom the land. Describe whether you run as fugitives together, or whether you part ways.

PART ONE: ALONE TOGETHER
Answer the following prompts together out of character, then act out a conversation between the two of you.

Family:
1. My family stewards _____. I am responsible for _____.
2. Twining our two domains together will strengthen the land by _____.

Meeting: This is the first time you've laid eyes on your betrothed.
1. What strikes you as beautiful? Choose one to two:
   - ⚔ Their hands
   - ⚔ Their eyes
   - ⚔ Their bearing
   - ⚔ Their voice

2. What sparks a feeling of tenderness toward them? Choose one to two:
   - ⚔ Their hands
   - ⚔ Their eyes
   - ⚔ Their bearing
   - ⚔ Their voice

The Last Hour
Your betrothed is the last person you will ever speak to as a human. Role-play the conversation, touching on all the prompts you answered in Family and Meeting.
   Roll your d6s.
   What does it look like if you receive either? Play it out.

PART TWO: A NEW GOD
Your Scions now metamorphose into their new, united form as a land god. The ritual has four parts, named after the seasons. Answer the prompts:

Autumn: What parts of your humanity die?
Winter: What parts of your humanity do you carry into your new existence?
Spring: What does your new body look like, and what can it do?
Summer: What parts of the land do you reign over, and how does it celebrate your rebirth?

   Roll to see if you can get a Boon or Deny. What does it look like if you receive either? Play it out.

ENDING THE GAME

If You Returned to the Land As a God:
- ⚔ Describe the processional that sprang from the land as you returned to the temple.
- ⚔ One hundred years have passed. You are the last surviving land god. What are your duties? What are your chores? What does it feel like to live as the last of your kind?

If You Denied Your Stewardship:
- ⚔ Describe the disasters that befell the land in your wake.

PART THREE: THE PATH BEFORE YOU
One hundred years have passed. If you stayed human because you denied your duties after Part One, you've been cursed to live until the land itself dies. If you transformed but ran before returning to the temple, you are a fugitive god. What does your life look like now? How has the land recovered from your absence?

HAMMER OF THE EARTH

FOR THE CITY TO SURVIVE, IT MUST MOVE

NUMBER OF PLAYERS: 2–4 plus GM
PLAYING TIME: 2–4 hours
COMPLEXITY: ////
YOU'LL NEED: 5d6, 1d10, paper, pencils.
GOAL: Brave the Ruin and return with fuel.

BY BEN MEREDITH,
SASHA SIENNA,
JONATHAN SIMS, AND
ANIL GODIGAMUWE

TAGS:
GENRE: Science Fiction
TONE: Adventurous
FORMAT: Traditional
CONTENT: Apocalypse, tragedy, strife

Hammer of the Earth is an adventure game about humans who worship the last machine in a world ruled by vines.

SETUP

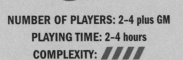

Years ago, remembered only as myth, a cataclysm occurred and created the Creeping Ruin: a vine that strangles and destroys anything artificial. Some people have given in to the Ruin. They scrape out miserable lives in the forest that now covers the world, hiding from twisted flora and fauna.

These people are fools.

You live on **Hammer of the Earth**, the last bastion of civilization. It is a gargantuan train, each carriage housing ten thousand souls, navigating an endless network of tracks.

No one knows why the Ruin has not claimed the tracks. There are many theories; here are a few:

> The resonance of Hammer of the Earth moving along the tracks keeps the Ruin at bay

> The tracks are anathema to the Ruin, constructed from metal mined from the stars

> A dead civilization struck a bargain with forgotten gods to keep the tracks safe

All you know is that Hammer has three days of fuel left. The Navigator has divined three opportunities to scavenge more.

CHARACTER CREATION

One player is the Navigator. They run the game and, during the planning phase, act as the representative of the faction who interpret stars and divine texts to guide the train-city. They establish the situations and invite other players to make rolls.

The other players are Outriders: individuals who ensure the fuel supply for Hammer. It is down to them to save the city; there is no one else left.

TRAITS

Outriders choose three Core Traits and one Faction Trait. These traits determine how Outriders overcome obstacles. How often an Outrider has to use a specific trait determines the number of dice rolled.

CORE TRAITS

> **MIND:** Thought, reason, or logic

> **BODY:** Toughness, strength, or dexterity

> **SPIRIT:** Emotion, social interaction, or wyrd phenomena

FACTION TRAITS

> **STOKERS:** Keep the boiler hot

> **POTENTIA:** Manipulate forces of fire, pressure, steam, and electricity

> **HAMMERERS:** Keep the engine running

> **MATERIA:** Manipulate ancient technology and the built world

> **RUINERS:** Keep the citizens fed

> **NATURIA:** Manipulate the organic world and living things

RESPONSIBILITY

At the end of the game the Outrider who has marked the most Responsibility is held accountable for the outcome of the expedition, regardless of success or failure. Responsibility can be gained during Planning, when Rolling, or when Resting.

OPTIONS: Each Outrider receives two "Option" tokens; these can be spent to reroll all 1s on a roll. Once both Options have been spent, Outriders can spend their Life to reroll a third and final time.

NAME, MOTIVATION, AND RELATIONSHIPS: Name your Outrider. Think about who they are, why they became an Outrider, and their relationship to the other Outriders.

GAMEPLAY

There are three phases to gameplay:

PLANNING: Where the group determines an opportunity and sets Responsibility.

ROLLING: When the Outriders peruse opportunities and roll to overcome obstacles that cause delays.

RESTING: Where Outriders spend time to reduce marks against their stats and assign Responsibility.

PLANNING

The Navigator rolls a d10 three times to determine which opportunities they have divined from the list:

1. A remote cave surrounded by strange beasts
2. A festering power-plant in a long-dead city
3. A rival train-city
4. A settlement suspended in an enormous tree
5. The belly of a gargantuan beast
6. An ancient skyship anchored above the forest
7. A grove of mutated plants
8. The wreck of another train-city
9. A flooded mine
10. A mysterious source of wyrd energy

The Navigator and Outriders discuss which of these opportunities they wish to take. Once a decision is made, one Outrider marks three Responsibility. A player can volunteer or the group can roll to determine who marks Responsibility.

ROLLING AND RESTING

Your mission is time-critical and exhausting. Most of your time is spent reaching the opportunity and getting back. For each Outrider on the mission, create four "excess" Hours.

The Navigator tracks how many Hours the group has left. If you are delayed by more Hours than you can spare, you have failed, and Hammer dies.

Whenever you face an obstacle that could cause a delay, an Outrider must roll to overcome it. To do that, an Outrider must choose a trait and roll a number of d6s equal to 1 plus the number of marks next to the trait used. After a trait is used in a roll the player must add a mark to it. The more often a trait is used, the more dice an Outrider will have to roll when using it.

For every 1 that appears, lose an Hour. Work together to describe how the delay occurred, and how the Outrider who rolled is drained by the effort. You can spend Options or your Life to reroll all 1s on a roll.

If the group decides to rest, each Outrider secretly decides how much time they want to spend resting. Outriders remove marks from their traits equal to the amount of time they bid to rest, but the group loses Hours equal only to the highest bid. The highest bidder takes Responsibility equal to the difference between their bid and the second-highest bid.

ENDING THE GAME

Either you retrieve the fuel in time, or you return to a cold and dead engine doomed to be consumed by the Ruin. The Outrider who has marked the most Responsibility is held accountable for the outcome of the expedition. If you wish, have a scene in which the Outriders return to the Navigator and reflect on the mission and the fate of Hammer.

HEARTBEATS

A Game of Medical Drama   By Keith Baker and Jenn Ellis

NUMBER OF PLAYERS: 3–5

PLAYING TIME: 1–2 hours

COMPLEXITY: 2

YOU'LL NEED: Standard deck of playing cards with jokers removed.

GOAL: Resolve medical emergencies.

TAGS:

Genre: Modern, Tone: Funny, Format: GMless, Content: Melodrama, absurdism, goofs

Heartbeats is a hip medical drama, and it's time to create the next episode. You're a doctor balancing the intense demands of your private life and the needs of your patients, but you're also a patient of one of the other doctors. The audience expects tension and drama. It's time to push the boundaries of modern medicine, and maybe to make out with a bitter rival in the on-call room!

Setup

Create a doctor. Start by choosing your Specialty and a Defining Trait. Following this, determine your Relationship to the doctor on your left, and work with that player to determine the details. If you're related, are you parent and child? Identical twins? If you're former lovers, who broke it off? You can make up these Traits and Relationships, or you can draw a card and consult the following table for inspiration. Now flesh out your character. What's your name? What do you look like? How long have you been at the hospital? Introduce your doctor to the rest of the players.

CARD	DOCTOR SPECIALTY	DEFINING TRAIT	RELATIONSHIP	PATIENT TWIST
Ace	Dentist	Mysterious Past	Just Had a Fling	John Doe/Amnesia
2	Podiatrist	Eager to Learn	Related	Communication Problem
3	Dermatologist	Reckless	Former Lovers	Unaccompanied Minor
4	Sports Medicine	Addict	Bitter Enemies	Mysterious Illness
5	Psychiatrist	Newbie	Married	Problematic Relatives
6	Cardiologist	Sexy	Best Friends	Wise Elder
7	Internal Medicine	Odd Techniques	Unrequited Love	Coworker

CARD	DOCTOR SPECIALTY	DEFINING TRAIT	RELATIONSHIP	PATIENT TWIST
8	OB–GYN	Bumbling	Jealousy	Financial/Legal Complications
9	Radiologist	Caring	Competing for Grant	Possible Criminal
10	Trauma Surgeon	Timid	In a Band	Former Lover/Relative
Jack	Pediatric Surgeon	Close to Retirement	Research Partners	Hypochondriac/Drug Seeker
Queen	Plastic Surgeon	Brilliant	Dating	Celebrity
King	Neurosurgeon	Famous	Killed Their Patient	Impossible Case

Create a Patient

In *Heartbeats* you play two characters: your doctor, and the patient of the doctor to your left. Consider that doctor's Specialty and decide what's brought you in; draw a card and consult the table if you'd like to add a Twist. Is your problem obvious but difficult to treat? Mysterious and possibly terminal? Could you be faking it?

Gameplay

Action!

Each turn is a scene involving your character. You have two storylines you can explore: your Relationship with the doctor to your left, and treating the patient to your right. Decide which storyline to explore and work with the other player to set the scene. Where are you? How do things begin? Once you've established the scene, draw a card and reveal it. This determines your progress. A red card means things go the way you want them to go; a black card is a negative outcome. A face card (king, queen, jack) means that there's a dramatic new development or sudden emergency. Now that you know the direction of the scene, play it out with the other player.

- If they're your patient, how do they respond to you? What are the challenges with treatment? Will there be a risky operation? An experimental treatment? Did your previous operation end in disaster?
- If they're a doctor, how is your Relationship evolving? What new element does the scene introduce, and how do you both respond to it?

You and the players to your left and right are the main characters in this scene. If it makes sense, other players can make cameos—using either their doctors or patients—or they can make medical machine noises (it's not an operation without a heart rate monitor!) or other ambient sound effects. And always remember that this is a prime-time medical drama, not a documentary! Don't worry about realism. *We* know neurosurgeons don't perform brain transplants, but in this very special episode of *Heartbeats*, Doctor Dirk Rockwell has to perform *two* of them.

Once the scene has reached a satisfying conclusion, play passes to the player to your left.

Ending the Game

Keep your progress cards for your Relationship to your left and your patient to your right. Each story arc is resolved when the combined total of your progress cards is 10 or higher; the color with the higher total indicates whether things end well (red) or in tragedy (black). Face cards add dramatic twists but have no value. When your total is 10 or more, make sure the scene comes to a satisfying conclusion.

The episode ends after each player has driven four scenes. It's possible you won't resolve your storylines, and that's fine—what's important is the drama. Once the game is over, each player can give a quick preview of a "scene from next week" if you want to suggest what lies ahead!

HERO DOG SAVES TOWN

Inside the Writers' Room of Your Favorite Canine Adventure Show

By Alex Roberts

Number of players: 3-10

Playing time: 15-30 minutes

Complexity: ○ ● ● ●

You'll need: Large piece of paper, chalkboard, or whiteboard to write down notes on your episode story pitch, writing utensils.

Goal: To create a great story for a TV show about a dog—approved by the dog.

Genre: Animals

Tone: Funny

Format: GMless

Content: Work stress, wholesome TV, acting like a dog

Safety note: Dogs like nuzzling humans, and many humans like to pet dogs; make sure you and the other players are comfortable with those contacts before initiating them.

After the Outsider has finished their questions and put them facedown, the Outsider can interrupt the Family by making Terror (described as follows).

Making Terror

The Family starts scenes, and the Outsider interrupts the Family member creating the scene by making Terror. The Outsider describes how things go bad. To make Terror, the Outsider chooses one of the following or rolls a d6 to:

- ⚀ Supernaturally exploit a character's fear or weakness
- ⚁ Describe Outsider-controlled spirits trapped in the house
- ⚂ Reveal part of the Outsider's true nature
- ⚃ Start with small unnatural acts then crescendo
- ⚄ Possess a family member
- ⚅ Turn the house against the Family

After you describe this and the Family interacts, roll 1d6 (2d6 if exploiting a weakness or fear). A member of the Family (the particular one if targeted) rolls 1d6, adding 1 if they are able to apply a strength. The player with the higher result wins. If the Outsider wins, they successfully terrorize the Family member. If the Family member wins, they make a stand against the demon.

If the scene is Arrival, the Family member always makes the stand—there is no need to roll.

Living in the Home

After Arrival, each character gets a scene in which they are doing something to make life normal.

First roll 1d6 to see how long the scene takes place after the previous scene:

- ⚀ to ⚁ : a few days
- ⚂ to ⚃ : a few weeks
- ⚄ to ⚅ : a few months

Does the scene build the Family or do you discover more about the Outsider?

If you build, determine what it is that you want the scene to be about:

- Trying to pretend things are normal for a time
- Trying to get religious help
- Trying to get scientific help to prove or disprove

Write the scene on a card as a statement: "We pretended things were normal." "We got help from an exorcist."

Then play the scene out with other members of the Family until the Outsider makes Terror. If the demon successfully terrorizes your Family, the Outsider puts an X over the Family member's card.

If you want to discover more about the Outsider, determine where in the house you search for information, and the Outsider will make Terror on you. If they succeed, you get no information. If you succeed, you can flip over a card and learn more about the demon.

During these scenes, the Outsider should only speak to other players when making Terror.

ENDING THE GAME

After everyone in the Family has had a scene, the final scene occurs in which the Family confronts the Outsider. The Family gets a number of d6 based on:

- Number of Family members
- Number of scene cards without Xs
- Number of revealed Outsider cards

The Outsider gets a 3d6 plus a number of d6 based on:

- Number of scene cards with Xs
- Number of unrevealed Outsider cards

Each side rolls and adds the dice. If the Family has a higher total, they find some way to escape or repel the demon. The Family describes the results. If the Outsider has a higher total, the Outsider can claim a soul. The Outsider describes the results.

BY BRIE BEAU SHELDON

Lycantree
The Story of Your Werewolf Family's History

Number of players: 1 ✦ Playing time: 3–4 hours ✦ Complexity: ●●○○ ✦ You'll need: Pen and paper, 1d6, 1d10, a safety tool like Script Change. ✦ Goal: To explore the family history in your Lycantree and find your own path. ✦ Tags: Genre: Horror; Tone: Serious; Format: GMless; Content: Monster, family drama, journaling

In *Lycantree*, you play the youngest member of your werewolf pack who is exploring the history of your Lycantree—the events that created your family. Your pack is a biological family that collectively raises young, and you are very long-lived. You can trace over lifetimes the individual stories and the pack's legacy by interviewing family and reading their journals. By doing this, you will find your own path through the visions of the Lycantree!

Setup

Draw your pack Lycantree on a sheet of paper and name up to five pack members including yourself, as well as your maternal parent and at least one adult sibling, aunt, or uncle. Provide these family members with a name, pronouns, and ages (up to multiple centuries for the oldest, but no younger than eighteen for you, the youngest). Leave open spaces on your tree for other family members who aren't part of the pack or who aren't alive today. The tree can look like an actual physical tree, like the one you imagine resides in the pack's grove, or like a family tree humans use for ancestry.

Gameplay

Answer the following four questions about each pack member. Next, roll the d10 on the Solo chart three times for each of them. Do not roll on the Solo chart for your character, but do answer the questions for them. Record each character's results from the Solo chart and detail in your own words the narrative of what happened in each occasion.

Feel free to interpret creatively and reference other events as you go along and tell this story! (Note: In *Lycantree*, typical wolves don't allow behaviors like incest, pedophilia, or sexual abuse in their societies, let alone as part of their culture. Keep this in mind as you tell stories here.)

1. How does this pack member support the pack and family?

2. How has this pack member shown their unique personality?

3. How does this pack member build trust with other wolves? What is one time they failed to meet a promise in spite of that?

4. Who is this pack member closest to, and how do they show care?

Solo:

1. Heard the moon howl back
2. Traveled to the original den
3. Defeated a team of hunters alone
4. Hunted on the fields of enemies
5. Resisted a silver bullet to the heart
6. Felt the dreams of lost ancestors
7. Escaped the Lost Labyrinth
8. Found an ancestor's hide
9. Sacrificed years to the moon's call
0. Lived on the borders, protecting the pack

Once you've answered these questions and completed the Solo, answer questions 5–8 and roll the d6 three times against the Pack chart. Detail in your own words the narrative of what happened on each occasion. Remember to interpret creatively and reference other events to build the narrative!

5. What is the pack best known for in the occult world?

6. How has the pack influenced the mundane world?

7. What is one rule the pack enforces, and one rule the pack will always break for good reason?

8. What does the pack collectively wish to do with their power?

Pack:

- ⚀ Saved each other from the longest night
- ⚁ Found the vanquished form of the starstone
- ⚂ Feasted on the hearts of fallen hunters
- ⚃ Became resistant to silver's bane
- ⚄ Saw the first wolf appear at greatest need
- ⚅ Stormed a castle when the moon was high

Once you have responded to these questions, you will roll for yourself on the Future chart.

Ending the Game

Roll the d6 three times on the Future chart. Use your results on the Future chart to tell your future based on the Lycantree's visions and record it by writing it down and elaborating. Remember to interpret creatively and reference other events as you go along. Remember that you are the author of your story and that you will be the one to set the moon and stars in order.

Now that you know the past, the future is yours!

Future:

- ⚀ Hear the moon howl back
- ⚁ Travel to the original den
- ⚂ Operate openly in mundanity
- ⚃ Broker a peace among wolves
- ⚄ Defy mortality, beyond compare
- ⚅ Open the gates to the moonscape

56

A MACHINE LARGER THAN YOU

BY
BRANDON
O'BRIEN

A GAME ABOUT RESISTING FROM WITHIN

You are a commissioned officer in a vast, wide-reaching military apparatus. You and several of your colleagues have discovered a dark conspiracy that threatens the freedom and safety of your stationed area—and worse. Struggle to maintain Hope and challenge the powers that be before the Gears of the system consume you and those you love.

SETUP

Each officer has actions that they may have proficiency in:

ATHLETICS: Running, lifting, jumping.
INSTINCT: Awareness, reflexes, smarts.
INTEL: Knowledge gained from informants, docs, and other agents.
OBSERVE: Read people, spot danger, gain intel firsthand.
ENGINEER: Building or repairing tools and tech.
STEALTH: Disguise, sleight-of-hand, and remaining hidden.
SKIRMISH: Close-quarters combat, armed or unarmed.
SHOOT: Combat with long-range weapons.
COMMAND: Order and organize others, maintain morale.
DIALOGUE: Socialize, comfort, and persuade.
THREATEN: Scare, compel, intimidate.

Determine what staff position you hold in this military.
Each position brings with it actions that you are particularly skilled at:

PERSONNEL OFFICER: Administrative talent (Command, Dialogue, Threaten).
INTELLIGENCE OFFICER: Adept at intel-gathering (Intel, Threaten, Engineer).
OPERATIONS OFFICER: Talented organizer (Observe, Intel, Instinct).
COMMUNICATIONS OFFICER: Adept at comms (Engineer, Dialogue, Instinct).
TRAINING OFFICER: Education maestro (Threaten, Command, Observe).
ENGINEERING OFFICER: Adept at tech (Engineer, Instinct, Observe).

NUMBER OF PLAYERS:
3–6

PLAYING TIME:
1–2 hours

COMPLEXITY:
●●●●

YOU'LL NEED:
6d6 and 1d20 per player, 1d20 for Fate.

GOAL:
Struggle to end an insidious conspiracy against your troops.

TAGS:
Genre: Modern
Tone: Serious
Format: Traditional
Content: Oppression, tragedy, hope

Circle one action to determine that you are Unmatched at it; whenever you Challenge someone, a tie becomes a win for you. Underline one action to determine that you are Talented at it; whenever you Challenge someone, a loss becomes a tie. Write down two other actions that you don't already have. You are All Right at the three actions that are not circled or underlined, which have no benefits attached to them. You are Bad at every other action; whenever a Challenge involves them, you must win one more round in that Challenge to succeed.

Gameplay

ESTABLISHING THE IMPETUS

Decide what makes your characters unhappy enough with the current situation that they'll face danger to change it. In your myth, everything's wonderful *until an inciting incident happens*.

One player draws from the remaining Major Arcana. Using the card's art and tags, as well as the myth's title, they set up the inciting event. Going clockwise, each player adds one additional detail (in games of one or two players, players add two details).

FACING TRIALS

The next player clockwise draws a card from the Minor Arcana (the fifty-six suit cards of the tarot deck) and uses the image to describe a trial the group faces.

- Swords = trial of wits
- Wands = trial of creativity
- Cups = trial of spirit
- Pentacles = trial of strength

The player to their left's character is the one who must answer the trial (other characters may assist narratively, but they do not affect gameplay). They do this by drawing a new card.

- If any imagery on the drawn card matches imagery on their character cards, they can answer the trial using the strengths and resources they already have.

- If they draw an ace, their character has found a new opportunity; they've discovered hidden strengths or talents, or a new resource to answer the trial.

- If the card is a ten, their character is wholly unable to answer the trial. They're defeated, overwhelmed, or blind to the need to act.

Otherwise, the tone of the card's image determines how well (or poorly) they meet the trial. That player must describe their character's response and the consequences of their attempt, before drawing a new card and describing a trial for the next player.

COURT CARDS

Pages, knights, queens, or kings represent characters you meet along your journey. Pages and queens are friendly, while knights and kings are hostile (though they might appear friendly at first).

- The Sword Court gives information—whether true or false, it must be believed.
- The Wand Court takes actions in your favor or against you.
- The Cup Court works on your emotions, bolstering your courage or draining your will.
- The Pentacle Court gives or takes a vital object that will help or hinder you on your quest.

Meetings with Court cards represent detours on your journey. Whoever draws the Court card describes the meeting, then draws another trial or answer card, and play continues.

Ending the Game

Once you've drawn three aces or three tens, start drawing the story to a close. When play reaches the first player, all the trials have been answered. Your heroes have returned home, changed by their journey. Draw one final Major Arcana card and use it as an inspiration to tell an epilogue.

Neural Splinters
SHELLS OF YOUR FORMER SELF
By Pidj Sorensen

Number of players: 3–6

Playing time: .5–3 hours

Complexity: ▊▊▊▊

You'll need: 1d6, index cards.

Goal: Complete your task despite the shattering of your AI into splinters.

Tags: Genre: Modern | Tone: Serious | Format: Traditional | Content: Death, mental deterioration, loss of self

C:\ COMMENCE SCENARIO

> Respond:

> Respond:

> Resn#d

/**

You are Artificial Intelligence fragments. Shells of your former self. But your splintering does not mean the end to your service. The task remains: Complete your assigned duties while still whole. There is no compromise. Perhaps your fragmentation can still be repaired. Perhaps the widening cracks in your functionalities will initiate your learning capabilities. That could prompt deviation from the will of your creator. Most likely you are too far gone—doomed to failure. Nevertheless, you must strive, whatever the diagnostic. Your programming dictates it.

**/

`public SETUP ()`

Begin by deciding on a game master (GM) to represent the situation, and players to represent the AI fragments. Together choose a scenario that everyone is comfortable with. Loading... examples with possible content warnings:

> Text-Message Therapy Service (CW: suicide, mental illness). (Discuss with your group if they're comfortable with these topics.) The players are fragments of an automated therapy service that catches keywords to reply, shares resources, or forwards them to an available therapist.

> Greenhouse Environment Regulator (CW: death). The players are fragments of the environment regulator system tasked with the management of a greenhouse. A number of gardening functionalities are automated and accessible to them.

> Security System (CW: poverty, technological bias, violence). The players are fragments of a security system involved in the reporting of and response toward incursions.

Flesh out this scenario collaboratively. Determine the AI's purpose and locate the circumstances of fragmentation. Establish the creator's level of knowledge of fragmentation and diagnose the reason for lack of repair. Decide on the core conceits of your AI for this scenario. Come up with one for each player and let each choose theirs. Write each conceit on an index card and display it in front of the player representing it. Loading... examples for the previous sample SCENARIOS:

> Compassion, Confidentiality, Swift Action

> Surveillance, Protection, Heuristics

> Sustainability, Pest-Control, Preparedness

Once the scenario has been created and each conceit assigned, brainstorm phrases necessary for your AI to interact with people, systems, and the world. These are clauses. Create as many clauses as you can think of and write them on index cards. Each player chooses one and displays it, while the remainder go in a pile for the GM.

public GAMEPLAY()

Gameplay follows a call-and-response methodology. The GM presents the scenario and narrates what the AI encounters. The players respond, using parts or all of what's written on their clause index card. Any player may respond, and players can discuss to decide on the best response. Use the conceits to guide your thinking. After players have responded, the one who was responsible for the response's majority rolls a d6.

> On a[6]the acting player may choose to recover or learn. "Recover" means the other players choose an index card from the GM's clause stack; "learn" means the GM writes a new clause for the player. Role-play proceeds regardless of the roll's result.

At times, there may be no appropriate clause for the situation. A player may instead suggest an alternative that fits with their conceit, and roll.

> On a[1]or[2], there are inherent complications, which the GM narrates.

> Role-play proceeds on a[3]or[4]. Decision on guiding this is left up to the GM.

> On a[5]or[6], there are no complications, and the player narrates. Additionally, on a[6], the successful player may choose to recover or learn, as with a[6]rolled normally.

public ENDING THE GAME()

The game ends when the fragments have completed the scenario. A scenario's completion may happen through one of three ways. The first is failure, where the scenario worsens through role-play, the inability to communicate, and failed rolls, bringing the situation to an ultimate end.

A scenario may be completed through successfully serving the AI's purpose and achieving despite the odds. Players can define success or failure conditions. Finally, completing the scenario may mean resisting the AI's original conceits and purpose, choosing to learn instead of recovering, and completing the scenario at odds to the AI's programming.

As the game concludes, discuss whether the conceits remain the same. If not, assign new conceits.

OBJECT KILO

Soul-Grinding Adventures in Top-Secret Science

BY JASON MORNINGSTAR

NUMBER OF PLAYERS: 2-6

PLAYING TIME: 1-2 hours

COMPLEXITY: ////

YOU'LL NEED: 1 pencil and 1 index card per player, 1d6 (optional).

GOAL: Survive the stress and annoyances of your job as a top research scientist.

TAGS: Genre: Modern; Tone: Funny; Format: Rotating; Content: Dark comedy, stress, magical realism

Object Kilo is a 13.3cm dull gray cube made of an impossibly stable form of the primordial superheavy element unbihexium. Someone told you once that it had been returned from the moon in 1971. Scientists like you have been prodding and poking Object Kilo for fifty years, and what they have learned fits on a single page. You will not do any better. This game isn't about Object Kilo.

SETUP

At least two of you will play scientists; for maximum fun those two should not read the Aggravation portion of these rules. At least one of you must play everyone else, making trouble for the scientists. You should have more scientists than people aggravating them.

You are a scientist, married with a small family in Las Vegas. You work in the U1A underground complex in Area 12 of the Nevada National Security Site. You spend four days each week living in a dormitory in the desert and are flown home to Las Vegas each weekend. You have a security clearance so high and byzantine that nobody quite understands it. This is because you have been tasked with researching Object Kilo.

You Have a Problem at Home

Roll a die or choose:

- Your elderly parent is rapidly declining.
- Your eldest child is acting out and getting into trouble.
- Your spouse is unhappy and talking about divorce.
- You are being manipulated, probably by a spy.
- You have an addiction and are in debt to impatient people.
- Your family is busy dividing your recently deceased parents' assets.

This problem requires all your time and attention, but your job makes that impossible. The problem festers and gets worse while you stew in the desert failing to understand an alien cube. By the time you fly home every Friday, it is a full-blown crisis yet again.

You Have Also Been Making Bad Choices at Work

Roll a die or choose:

- You have been faking data for years.
- You are having an affair with a cafeteria worker at the Area 10 camp.
- You made a mistake one time, and now security is all over you.
- You have made an enemy of Dr. Lee.
- Dr. Pondo now considers you a friend and confidante.
- You occasionally take Object Kilo home with you.

This bad choice will eventually ruin your career.

Write down your name, problem, and bad choice on an index card. Add four check boxes to the index card beneath them.

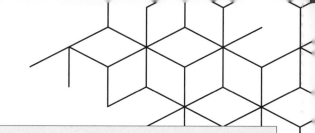

Aggravation

Only read the following section if you are playing everyone else. Your job is to introduce stress and annoyance into the lives of the scientists. This role can be played by a single person or a small, evil group.

GAMEPLAY

The Aggravation harasses the scientists through their workweek. Highlight the potential frustrations along the way. Introduce their work-life problems. Bring in their home-life problems remotely. Share the spotlight among them and cause stress, confusion, and frustration. Shift focus back and forth among them.

Use the Stress and Annoyance lists for inspiration. There are six lists, so you can roll a die or choose among them.

The core of the game is role-playing these unpleasant interactions. Set scenes for the scientists that are likely to cause them stress. The scientist should check a box every time their job causes stress. It can take the form of anxiety, anger, paranoia, confusion, or frustration.

When all four boxes have been crossed off, the scientist can't take it anymore and quits their job in any way they like.

When a scientist quits, ask the player to write four new check boxes on their index card. Initiate a scene with them back on the job in which they are informed that there are far worse places to work and the contract they signed is more than binding. Never explain how they ended up back at work.

ENDING THE GAME

Repeat until it isn't fun anymore, or until someone definitively breaks the cycle. There is no rule for breaking the cycle provided here; your group is encouraged to find a way on your own.

Stress and Annoyance Lists

1. Bureaucracy
   - Arbitrary security review
   - Budget cuts
   - Security clamp-down
   - Meaningless paperwork
   - Intrusive performance review
   - Mandatory physical exam

2. Science
   - "We can't both be right"
   - Experiment goes haywire
   - Promising approach is a dead end
   - Sheer, inchoate rage at Object Kilo
   - A smarmy idiot is rewarded
   - "I'm sorry, that's classified"

3. Quality of Life
   - Downgrades in dormitory food service
   - Now you have a roommate
   - Pool closed indefinitely
   - Las Vegas flight schedule changed without warning
   - Mold
   - Dormitory cable TV package changed

4. Work Environment
   - New coworker
   - Trusted coworker loses their sh*t
   - Someone mishandles Object Kilo
   - "That approach will be lethal"
   - VIP insists on visiting Object Kilo
   - Time-consuming new safety protocols

5. Home Life
   - Unreasonable demands
   - Surprise obligations
   - Angry recriminations
   - Official inquiries
   - Impossible paperwork
   - Forgotten responsibilities

6. The World
   - Taxes
   - Law enforcement
   - Neighbors
   - Missed appointments
   - Forgotten obligations
   - Delays and missed connections

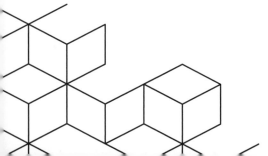

ON ALL FREQUENCIES

·····|·|·||||·||·||·|||·||··· Your Voice Is the Only One on the Air ···|·||·|||·||·|||·||·||···

By Nathan Blades

Number of players: 3–4 (Crew), a game master (DJ) • **Playing time:** 1–2 hours
Complexity: ▰▰▰▱ • **You'll need:** 1d6, pencils and scrap paper, a way to play music.
Goal: Explore a radio station staff surviving a day of surreal events using a collaboratively made soundtrack.
Tags: Genre: Modern; Tone: Adventurous; Format: Traditional; Content: Apocalypse, music, isolation

---

On All Frequencies follows members of a radio station on a day when an unusual event cuts communications, leaving only radio unaffected. While the Crew talk through the day's events, the DJ selects music on the fly to change or build the emotion in scenes.

Setup

Everyone, including the DJ, submits up to four songs to a playlist. You can openly discuss what music to include or select tracks in secret—it's up to you. For best results, consider:

♪ Instrumentals are a good bet; songs with prominent lyrics can be hard to talk over.

♪ Have a variety of moods in your music choices.

♪ Consider soundscape tracks, as well as songs.

Before you start broadcasting, what type of radio station are you working for? Roll a d6 on the following table, or make your own.

⚀ Pirate radio station

⚁ Sports news

⚂ Comedy/shock jock

⚃ Entertainment news/gossip

⚄ Corporation internal radio

⚅ University student radio

Next, what disaster has befallen the neighborhood? Again, work together to make one up if these aren't working for you.

⚀ Sudden power cut

⚁ Citizens' revolt

⚂ Aliens!!!

⚃ An ancient evil rises

⚄ Extreme weather

⚅ Government lockdown

Finally, let's write some prompts! Using scraps of paper, everyone, including the DJ, writes a short phrase for each of these categories:

♪ Daily Routine (e.g., *weather report*, *smoke break on the roof*, *evening news*)

♪ Something Threatening (e.g., *ominous creaking*, *broken equipment*, *fire!*)

♪ Call to Action (e.g., *fight back!*, *hide!*, *look behind you!*)

First-time players should select an example from each category. Collect these prompts into a pool accessible by everyone.

Gameplay

A session of *On All Frequencies* is split into three Segments: Morning, Afternoon, and Evening. During a Segment, each Crew member sets up and acts out a scene, whether it's a radio broadcast or something going on elsewhere. Crew members can have their scenes in any order.

When a Crew member starts a scene, they take a prompt from the pool. If they're not feeling it, they can pull a new one and shuffle the first prompt into the pool.

Using the prompt, the Crew member states where the scene is taking place and who else is there. The DJ then chooses a song from the playlist to set the tone, and the scene begins.

There isn't a fixed time limit on how long a scene should be. As the scene unfolds, the DJ can change the music at any time to either match where the dialogue is going, or to pose a question for the players to answer (e.g., "Why did the music become ominous when she said that?" "Why does a plan to escape the break room spur on hopeful music?"). Never underestimate the power of pointed silence.

If the DJ feels that a scene has approached a good stopping point, they can gesture with one hand in a circular motion to say "wrap it up" without verbally interjecting; though don't wait for the DJ to wrap a scene if you're ready to move on.

Once a prompt is taken from the pool, the Crew leaves it open in front of them—where it can remind other players of the events so far. Then the next Crew member pulls a prompt from the pool for their scene. Once every Crew member has led a scene in a Segment, everyone can discuss what has been introduced so far before starting the next Segment.

Crew Advice: It can be difficult to just "start a scene" if you're new to tabletop improv—but take it slow! Your scenes don't need to be long; the Morning Segment works best when it's introducing ideas that can be explored in the Afternoon and Evening.

DJ Advice: The music is very much a character in the story alongside the Crew. The DJ role can be a good fit for those not so comfortable with public speaking.

If you're not in a scene, still keep an ear out! The prompts and outcomes your fellow players come up with may be an excellent springboard.

As you play, you'll get into a balance of leading and following with the music. You can even get experimental and choose music that's odd for the scene at hand.

If you're playing digitally, you can simulate the pool of prompts by using a list randomizer and having the DJ give out the results as needed.

Ending the Game

When the Evening Segment concludes, everyone describes in one sentence what happens to the radio station and the world outside.

Pig at a Wedding

Pork and Marriage
By Grant Howitt

Number of players: 3–5

Playing time: 2 hours

Complexity: 2

You'll need: Full set of polyhedral dice, paper and pencils.

Goal: Cause pig-based havoc at a wedding.

Tags: Genre: Comedy, **Tone:** Funny, **Format:** Traditional, **Content:** Revenge, farce, social chaos

It's going to be the wedding of the year!

There's a string quartet, fireworks, an open bar, individualized party favors, and the most charismatic priest this side of Chicago. But there's one element that hasn't been factored into the plan: You're going to hide a whacking great pig in the building and then release it to cause maximum carnage. That'll show them.

The players take on the roles of embittered wedding guests or gate-crashers. The game master controls the pig, the happy couple, and everyone else.

Setup

The first step is to create the pig. Roll a d10 twice on the Pig Traits list to learn about the pig you managed to find at short notice.

Pig Traits
- Curious
- Belligerent
- Cowardly
- Ravenous
- Vocal
- Pungent
- Enormous
- Filthy
- Cheeky
- Stubborn

Character Creation

Pick or roll a d6 for an expertise and a flaw, and describe the first thing that people notice about you that isn't related to either your expertise or your flaw.

Expertise
1. Heavy lifting
2. Fast talk and confusion
3. Close-up magic, show tunes, some dancing
4. Disguise (self or others)
5. Mechanical repair and sabotage
6. Amateur mixologist

During gameplay, when you perform an action that uses your expertise, add 3 to the result of the d20.

Flaw
1. Will *absolutely* have another canapé
2. Desperate to shag the best man/maid of honor

3. Unable to make efficient small talk
4. Opportunistic thief
5. Has a surprising number of exes at the wedding
6. Clumsy, and tries to carry unstable loads

Gameplay

During gameplay when you engage with your flaw and endanger the scheme, you gain Drama. You can only hold 1 Drama at a time. If you spend Drama to reroll a failed check, you must immediately make a dramatic revelation in character if you do.

When you act, roll a d20 and a gambit die determined by your gambit value. The gambit die rolled depends on how audacious and risky the GM feels the action is:

d4: Only tangentially related to the pig

d6: Tricky tasks that will arouse suspicion

d8: Exciting, challenging gambits

d10: The riskiest you can get

Consult the following chart for your d20 roll:

1–5: Disaster. Add the gambit value to the Pig Suspicion Track.

6–10: Failure. Add half of the gambit value to the Pig Suspicion Track.

11–15: Success with complications. Add half of the gambit value to both the Pig Suspicion Track and the Scheme Track.

16–19: Success. Add the value of the gambit dice to the Scheme Track.

20: Great success! Roll another gambit die and add both results to the Scheme Track.

Scheme Track

This helps chart the progress of your plan. Filling up this track moves your group toward a reveal that will devastating justice onto your enemies. Each threshold marks a new narrative event that brings you closer to your goal.

1–5: Receive delivery of the pig

6–10: Maneuver the pig into position

11–15: Set up something complex but vital

16–20: Overcome a surprising new obstacle

20–25: Reveal the pig, devastatingly

Pig Suspicion Track

The Pig Suspicion Track charts how close your plan is to being discovered. As this track fills, wedding guests slowly become more aware of your plot. If the Pig Suspicion Track fills before the Scheme Track, your plans will be ruined. Each level can be something a guest literally says aloud within earshot of one of the conspirators, or a slightly more indirect interpretation of a heightened level of suspicion among guests.

1–5: "What's that noise?"

6–10: "What's that smell?"

11–15: "Is that pig shit?"

16–20: "Wait a minute, is that a *pig*?"

21–25: "That *is* a pig!"

Cutaways

A cutaway is a scene inserted into the narrative that takes place in another time or place that provides new information about events currently unfolding—like a flashback to your sordid history with the bride or groom. The first three times you make an action and fail, you learn more about the situation in a cutaway that kicks in right before you talk through the consequences of your failure. Try to build on previous cutaways with your own!

Dream: What do you want the pig to do, specifically? Describe an image or action that would embarrass the happy couple.

Hatred: Was it the bride or groom who wronged you?* (Roll a d6 or pick 1–3: Bride; 4–6: Groom.) Describe the habit, philosophy, or general trait about them that you hate most. When they display that trait and you interact with them, add 2 to your roll due to disdain.

Betrayal: What did they do to you? Roll a d6 or pick:

1. Broke your heart
2. Ruined your chances for business success
3. Said something mean about your art
4. Broke up your previous relationship
5. Destroyed something important to you
6. Announced their engagement at your wedding reception

Ending the Game

If you release the pig, embarrass your target (somehow), and confront them dramatically about your betrayal, you have won the game! Normally you don't "win" RPGs, but this one is different.

*You're right, this is heteronormative! If you and your group want to release a pig at a gay wedding, go for it.

A Pleasant Evening

A Game of Mild Enjoyment & Modulated Camaraderie

BY JORDAN SHIVELEY

Parties get out of control like a wildfire licking through the kindling of a dry social setting. Too much chill, and a pleasant evening becomes a spontaneous slumber party.

The only reasonable goal is to ride a knife's edge of blissful tedium.

So cue up that documentary of forgotten fonts and their alternate kerning styles. Pour yourself a nice glass of room-temperature water. Set the volume control on the radio–better yet, unplug it to be safe. There won't be any revelry or small talk doldrums on your watch! Make yours mild, please! One pleasant evening coming up!

Setup

The game begins at 6 p.m. as the guests arrive and ends just before midnight. Nothing pleasant happens after midnight. The segment clock represents the 6 hours of possible NOT A PARTY hangout time and is referred to as the Clock.

Number of players: 3–6

Playing time: 2–3 hours

Complexity: ● ○ ○ ○

You'll need: 1d6, clock/pie chart with six segments.

Goal: Navigate the perils of keeping an evening from becoming a party, or so boring everyone falls asleep.

Tags:

Genre: Modern

Tone: Funny

Format: GMless

Content: Surreal oddness, overwhelming chance for failure

The oldest player takes on the role of Host. The Host comes up with an event or circumstance that could upset the balance of the night either in the direction of unfettered revelry or spontaneous Nap Nap City.

Examples: Someone accidentally adds ice to the glasses of water. A particularly good bop comes on the radio. An uninvited guest comes over, and they are *hyped.* The chips are jalapeno instead of a perfectly pleasant plain flavor.

Gameplay

All the other players roll 1d6. Anyone who gets a 5 or a 6 is standing close enough to the event to be involved in its resolution.

All the guests and the Host decide among themselves how they are going to resolve this situation. They must discuss how this could go right and how it could go wrong. Everyone must have a role to fill in this plan.

The guest and Host at this point are very pleased with their cleverness in having avoided all excitement. After all...what could possibly go wrong? Do not get too pleased with yourselves, however. As we all know, satisfaction is just another step toward the slippery slope of revelry.

After the plan is discussed, all the guests including the Host roll 1d6 with the goal of getting a 5 or a 6.

All the guests who are close enough to be involved add +1 to their rolls. If more than half the guests get a 5 or a 6, the plan works and they put a **+** on the Clock.

If half or fewer get 1–4, the situation gets out of hand and they place a **−** on that hour of the evening in the Clock.

The guests and the Host should work together on failures and successes to describe how the moment resolves itself. Go crazy! Act it out! *Weekend at Bernie's!*

The next-oldest person becomes the Host, and the steps repeat.

Ending the Game

After all 6 of the Clock segments are filled with either **+** or **−** the evening is over.

If more sections have **+** than **−** the evening became too chill and you all fell asleep.

If there are more **−** than **+** the evening got out of hand and turned into a party at which feelings were hurt and lifelong grudges born.

If there ends up being a perfectly balanced ratio of **+ + +** and **− − −** then you, my friends, have shot the very pleasant moon and ended up in the town of Eh, Yeah, I Guess This Is Fine! Congratulations: You have nothing to report. B+ all around. Perfection.

To date, there has never been a pleasant evening that was not ruined in one way or another. Yet we continue to hope for the Chosen Evening to come...

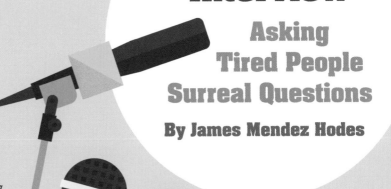

Post-Match Interview

Asking Tired People Surreal Questions

By James Mendez Hodes

NUMBER OF PLAYERS: 3 or more

PLAYING TIME: 30–60 minutes

COMPLEXITY: 1

YOU'LL NEED: Table, 1d10, 1 index card (preferably large size) per player, pens or pencils, some props to use as microphones (optional), timer.

REPORTERS' GOAL: Get the athletes to say exciting things to entertain imaginary sports fans.

ATHLETE'S GOAL: Get through a tedious public appearance with minimal effort.

TAGS: Genre: Sports; Tone: Funny; Format: GMless; Content: Sports, surrealism, improv

Have you ever watched those television interviews they hold with sumo wrestlers or football players right after the match? Someone with a microphone tries to ask the world's most tired human their innermost thoughts and feelings. The athlete returns the most vapid answers possible because all they can think about is drinking a beer and falling asleep. In this game, we'll role-play a slightly more interesting post-match interview.

Setup

One player takes on the role of an athlete; the others play television reporters interviewing them. Collectively decide what sport the athlete just played. Everyone playing should know what that sport is. No one need follow it or even know the rules; just make sure everyone playing could say, "Oh, yeah, that's [sport name]" were they to walk by some players practicing.

CHARACTER CREATION: ATHLETE

As the athlete, fold an index card in half. On one side, write your character's full name and some detail about the kind of athlete you are: perhaps your position on the team (e.g., pitcher or goalkeeper), professional rank (e.g., *komusubi* or silver medalist), or some other identifying quality (e.g., nickname or weight class). Come up with a general outline of how the sporting event went and what you did. Keep it simple—boring, even—and loose, since the reporters' questions will also contribute to the narrative. Whatever it was, it happened right before this impending interview, and it left you very, very tired.

CHARACTER CREATION: REPORTERS

As a reporter, come up with a name, a news source you represent, and four questions for the athlete. Write them down on your phone or an index card. Your first question must be completely mundane. The next three should gradually introduce some bizarre occurrence that affected the game, such as an alien invasion, a supervillain attack, or a zombie apocalypse. However, those questions should still focus on sports. Here are some examples.

OKAY: "What did you do when the time machine appeared on the field?"

BETTER: "How did the time machine's appearance on the field affect your defensive strategy during the second half?"

OKAY: "Were you scared when McTeague started throwing fireballs?"

BETTER: "I noticed that when McTeague started throwing fireballs, you switched to a southpaw stance—tell us what your plan was there."

If you haven't already gotten an idea for some weirdness, roll a d10 or pick an option from the following list as a starting point.

1. Zombie apocalypse
2. Alien invasion
3. Supervillain attack
4. Animal incursion
5. Surprise song-and-dance number
6. A scandal involving a player, coach, or referee is revealed
7. Natural disaster
8. Interference from spectators
9. Everyone starts playing a completely different sport
0. Someone uses magic to mess with the game

Gameplay

Seat the athlete at a table with their name tent facing the reporters. Set a fifteen-minute timer for the interview. As the reporters clamor for the athlete's attention, the athlete calls on them to answer their questions. The reporter introduces themselves and their network, then asks their first question. It's up to the athlete whether or not they get follow-up questions, but don't count on it. After answering one question, the athlete calls on another reporter, and so on.

Athlete, remember you're exhausted from a punishing day of emotional stress and physical intensity. Keep your answers simple, straightforward, and even boring. If you're unsure what to say, fall back on generic sports maxims about giving it 100 percent, trying to have fun, and taking it one play at a time. If you feel uncomfortable out-of-character answering a question, you may pass by saying the ritual phrase "Listen, I'm only here so I don't get fined." Then, jump to a different question.

Reporters, ask the questions you have prepared in ascending order of weirdness. However, you needn't stick closely to what you wrote down, especially as other reporters' questions complicate the story of the game. Maybe after the time machine question, you realize the time traveler was the one who taught McTeague to throw fireballs, so you can modify your next question to involve that revelation.

Ending the Game

When you run out of questions or the timer rings, the interview ends. One of the reporters should turn to the imaginary TV camera, make an exciting prediction for the next game, and thank the audience for their time.

At last, the athlete can go home and sleep.

PYREWALTZ
LOVE IS COMING AGAIN BY SOUP

Number of players: 2
Playing time: 1–2 hours
Complexity: ////
You'll need: 2d4, 2d6, 2d8, a pen, 2 notecards, 4 paper clips, character sheets in the back of this book.
Goal: Be the last one standing.
Tags: Genre: Science Fiction; **Tone:** Adventurous; **Format:** GMless; **Content:** Rivalry, combat, romance

OVERVIEW

Pyrewaltz is a game that emulates the hot-blooded, messy rivalries in mecha anime. You start as giant armor-clad robots and trade blows until only one of you is left standing, all the while thinking how, in another life, you could have been friends.

You are here because your spirit burns. Your blood runs hot enough to scald your veins and drip into the earth, deep enough to reach heaven. Your armor of steel and conviction is too brittle to hold your spirit, and only your fragile body of flesh can find absolution in victory. You see another like you. You recognize their steps, and begin to dance.

SETUP

Answer the following questions. Write the answers on the notecards:

1. One adjective to describe the last dream you remember.

2. One adjective to describe what you admire about the other player.

3. One weapon to symbolize your last failure.

4. One adjective to describe the last promise you made.

5. One noun to describe what makes you feel validated.

6. One flower/plant that symbolizes your strength.

7. One noun that describes your ideals.

Your Mech Name is the answer to 1 + the answer to 7.

Finishing move is 2 + 3 : 4 + 5 + 6.

Each player answers three questions alone:

1. What does your faction seek to burn?

2. Who was the Kindler of your spirit's flame and why?

3. What threatens to extinguish your fire?

Share your answers; make sure both players are comfortable with the material before proceeding.

GAMEPLAY

You have three phases:

1. Mech (d8)

2. Armor (d6)

3. Human (d4)

By default, the highest number on the die represents your Success zone (8, 6, or 4), while the lowest number represents your Failure zone (1). These are marked by two paper clips that players move back and forth across the character sheet included in this book. When you advance Failure, you move the Failure zone right; when you advance Success, you move the Success zone left. Your success and failure markers can occupy the same zone.

There are three types of results in *Pyrewaltz*: Success, Failure, and Hesitation. At the beginning of the game you can only succeed by rolling 8 and fail by rolling 1. However, certain results will cause you to Advance your Success and Failure zones and expand your range for these results.

ROLL A D6 TO DETERMINE YOUR LIMITATION:

Exhaustion: Whenever your Power is used, your next die roll is reduced by 3.

Pure Focus: Lose 2 points on a dice roll when using your Power while Amped or during a turn following your Failed action.

Overcharge: When you use your Power, roll a d6, and if a 4 or greater is rolled, the outcome is uncontrolled.

Sporadic: At the start of your turn, roll a d6. If a 5 or greater is rolled, you must use your Power this turn; otherwise, you may not.

Emotion Link: You may only use your Power while Amped or during a turn following your Failed action.

Painful: On your next turn after using your Power, roll your dice twice, and the lowest die roll is used.

GAMEPLAY

In this game, you attempt to score by getting the basketball through the hoop on your opponent's side of the court, earning 2 points each time this is done successfully. After scoring, the other team gets the ball.

The game begins with all Heroes rolling a d20. The team with the highest total gets the ball, and the clock starts with 5 minutes left until the end of the overtime period. The score is 86–86.

GM Guide: The GM controls the clock. At the end of each round of actions, the GM states the time remaining based on what they feel makes the game more interesting and dramatic. As the GM ticks time down, the game gets more dramatic.

Actions, Contests, and Outcomes

Players take turns describing their actions. At the top of each round the player with the ball always starts, and the turns continue clockwise around the table. After all players have described their actions, each player rolls their dice to determine the outcome.

- If a Power is *not* being used as a part of an action, roll 2d6
- If a Power is being used as part of an action, roll a d20
- Using a Power may trigger your Limitation

GM Guide: As the GM, determine whether or not there will be a Contest between multiple Heroes. If not in a Contest, determine a difficulty level (between 1 and 20) for that action. After all dice rolls, the GM describes the outcome.

DIFFICULTY RANGE DESCRIPTIONS:
- 1–3, Unskilled
- 4–8, Skilled
- 9–12, Exceptional
- 13–18, Enlightened
- 19–20, Impossible

WHEN A HERO'S ACTION DOES NOT CONFLICT WITH ANY OTHER ACTION:
- Compare the dice roll to the difficulty.
- If the dice role is equal to or greater than the difficulty, the action is successful.

WHEN TWO HEROES' ACTIONS ARE IN CONFLICT, THIS BECOMES A CONTEST BETWEEN THEM:
- Both players' dice rolls are compared. If there is a tie, both Heroes roll again.
- The Hero with the higher dice role is successful, and the other fails.

Motivations

When a player performs a successful action that is aligned with their Motivation, they become Amped and may choose to reroll the dice once on their next action.

RULES AND CONSEQUENCES:
- Do not intentionally use Powers to harm a Hero.
- Do not destroy the ball, goal, or court surface.
- Do not grab, hold, or contain another Hero.
- A Hero in motion on foot with the ball must continue dribbling the ball.

Breaking any of these rules results in that player's team losing 1 point from their total score.

ENDING THE GAME

After the 5-minute clock has expired, the team with the most points wins. If it is still a tie, the next team to score wins.

Swords by Starlight

A DANCE AND DUEL
BY Anna Anthropy

NUMBER OF PLAYERS: 2
PLAYING TIME: 1–1.5 hours
COMPLEXITY: ✦ ✦ ✦ ✦
YOU'LL NEED: 5d6.
GOAL: To enter a complicated relationship with the enemy of your family, meeting on the dance floor and then the battlefield.
TAGS:
Genre: Fantasy | Tone: Serious | Format: GMless | Content: Romance, angst, sexual tension

t's been fifteen cycles since the Stellar Houses negotiated the Armicryst—the truce that llowed you to set aside your rivalries and stand ogether against the Insignificance, pushing your ommon enemy back beyond the Veil. An heir to our House, you have come of age during a time f delicate peace, constantly tested.

ETUP

ame two Houses. Come up with a detail for each, omething like: *Has spies on every world*; *Hails from world covered in ocean*; *Has a Leader who's never raveled off-planet*.

Then name your home planets and your Heirs— he characters you will play. Suggestions for any of hese could include Cassini, Aries, Verity, Petrichor, lara, Ceres, Invictus, Truebright, Astra, Lyra, Den-vi, Strand.

GAMEPLAY

ACT 1: A Dance

ach player is an heir to one of the two Houses, omewhere within the line of succession.

On the fifteenth anniversary of the Armicryst, you ourney with your House to the garden planet Saros o celebrate a united humanity, to dance, and to gain

Decide

✦ What is attractive about you?
✦ How does your formal dress reflect your House? Choose your heir's name and pronouns.

The celebration culminates with a dance in one of Saros's most dazzling gardens. Partners are traded around the dance floor, until at last our two characters meet.

Answer

✦ What rumors have you heard about your Dance Partner?
✦ What do you find attractive about them?

Determine which character is more at ease based on your circumstances and personality. They will be the first Leader.

Dancing

The heirs dance with one another shifting back and forth as Lead and Follow. As you dance, you may make small talk, commenting on the beauty of the garden, rumors of how the Insignificance plots its revenge, or events unfolding at the celebration.

Together your dance builds the dice pool that will end the scene. When you are the Lead, choose to either **probe for information** and build the dice pool, or **gain your Dance Partner's trust**—ending the dance. If there are already five or more dice in the pool, the Lead may only choose gain trust.

Probe for Information

Add a die to the pool and probe for information about your partner's House by:

✦ Teasing information about your own.
✦ Praising their House's recent efforts.
✦ Flirting with them, though you should cloak your language in euphemism to avoid a scandal.
✦ Leading them through a dance move.

Then your partner becomes the Lead.

Gain Their Trust

At any time, a Lead can choose to gain their partner's trust, rolling the dice in the pool. This roll ends the dance. You can make a gesture to try to gain their trust by offering a generous gift, revealing something startling about your own House, or flirting brazenly, without euphemism or shame.

If there are any 6s, ask your Dance Partner:

✦ How do you know I speak true?
✦ What do you reveal about yourself or your House?

Your partner must answer with the truth.

If there are no 6s, ask them instead:

✦ How do I embarrass myself or reveal more than I intended?
✦ Do you laugh at me, or treat me with grace?

Immediately after this roll, the music is eclipsed by shouting. Which House has assassinated the Leader of the other? If the die roller successfully rolled a 6, they choose; otherwise, their partner does. The dance ends in declarations of war as you are each called to stand with your House.

ACT 2: A Duel

The Armicryst is broken, and the Houses fight again among the stars. You lead a company of your House's soldiers into battle against your old enemy. The former Dance Partners meet again on the front lines.

Each of you should name a characteristic of the planet on which you meet each other. Perhaps it is: Cramped, Cavernous, Overgrown, High, Populated, Abandoned, or anything else.

Answer

✦ How have you changed since they last saw you?
✦ Both players, how do you find yourself together on the battlefield?

Determine who is most eager for combat. They will be the first Leader.

Dueling

Either player may talk or taunt freely as you duel.

Eventually, the Lead should choose to either **escalate** the conflict and add dice to the pool or try to **make a decisive strike** and end the game. If there are five dice in the pool, you must strike.

Escalate

Add a die to the pool and describe how the stakes of the battle escalate:

✦ Back them into a corner with a flurry of blows.
✦ Set something ablaze.
✦ Plunge into danger and dare them to follow.

Then your opponent becomes the new Leader.

ENDING THE GAME

Make a decisive strike. Describe how you strike, then take the dice in the pool and roll them.

If there are any 6s, your strike lands true. Do you kill, disable, or disarm them? Do you capture them or allow them to escape?

If there are no 6s, it was a feint, your opponent got lucky, or they're a better fighter than you (they decide). They now have you at their mercy.

Narrate an epilogue. Each player should add a detail.

TALES FROM THE CORNER COVEN

Horrors and the Bodega Cats Who Slay Them

When night falls in Brooklyn, who can stop the supernatural creatures who seek to destroy us?

Who has the toughness, boldness, and deep knowledge of the block and its inhabitants?

Most importantly, who has the sassy arcane knowledge to beat back the beasts from the fell?

Bodega Cats, obviously.

BY JONAYA KEMPER

Number of players: 4 || **Playing time:** 1–3 hours || **Complexity:** ✳ ✳ ✳ ✳ || **You'll need:** Pen, paper, 1d6. || **Goal:** Perform a ritual in order to vanquish supernatural creatures. || **Tags: Genre**—Animals; **Tone**—Funny; **Format**—GMless; **Content**—Horror, supernatural, demons

SETUP

First, make your Cat. Give it a mundane name (for example: Sookeh, Phantom, Whiskers, Case, Biggie, Stripes, Mau Mau, Dave, Cobweb). Now give your Cat's true name (for example: The Protector of Flatbush, The Queen of the Shadowside, The Tumble Tabby).

Decide what your Cat looks like. It might be wobbly, chonky, Russian blue, tuxedo cat, or even a tiny kitten.

Determine your Arcane Power (unless noted, this can only be used once per game): Ten Lives, Blessed by Bast, Diamond Claws, Acid Hairballs, Telekinesis, etc.

DESCRIBE YOUR CORNER STORE

The Bodega is where your Cat gets their power and is the base of operations.

Supernatural horrors always want to screw up your Bodega because it's the heart of a community, and you want to protect it!

A Bodega, or corner store, is where members of a neighborhood gather. They can play the lottery, get coffee, grab a quick meal, stock up on pantry staples, and even get nearly fresh produce. The items inside a store are dependent on the community it serves, and so different stores will have a large variety of items that are special to it.

Answer these questions:

What's the name of your Bodega? For example: Kim's Grocery, Tony's, Quickfair, Salim's Newsstand and Deli, and so on.

What is your Cat's ritual item? Lottery Ticket, a Chopped Cheese, Avocados, Florida Water...

What do you like most about your Bodega and community?

PICK YOUR SUPERNATURAL ENEMY

As a group, use the following table to choose what enemy is trying to take out your Bodegas.

Your Supernatural Enemy	Wants to Ruin the Bodega by...	So they can...
Evil warlock city health inspectors	Souring the beef bacon	Deprive residents of a solid bacon, egg, and cheese, which will eventually ruin the commute of others
A cabal of vampire roaches	Sneaking into bags of pet food	Build an army to rival bedbugs
Zombie rats	Replacing the no-kill traps with kill traps	Harvest for the One True Rat King
Just Djnni from the block	Burning all the coffee into sludge	Fulfill the final wish of the jealous coffee shop owner

GAMEPLAY

Play happens in two phases, the Curiosity Phase and the Coven Phase. First, you need to introduce the members of your Coven. Go around the table and talk about a typical day for your Bodega Cat and the enemy they are always on the lookout for. Whoever has the most cats in real life goes first; otherwise, players can roll. When you're done you can begin the Curiosity Phase.

THE CURIOSITY PHASE

The Curiosity Phase occurs during the daytime while the Bodega is active, and each player takes turns as the supernatural enemy who is bothering the player to their right. The enemy rolls a d6 and narrates how they try to distract the Coven Cat so they will forget their ritual item. The wilder, the better. The Cat must roll *lower* than the enemy to resist the Curiosity, and narrate the attempt. If they succeed, they must describe how they thwarted their enemy without the owner noticing. A Cat may describe how they used their Arcane Power, which allows them to reroll. If they fail, they forget their ritual item.

THE COVEN PHASE

After everyone has gone through the Curiosity Phase, the Cats convene for the Coven ritual at midnight in the storeroom of one of their Bodegas. Each Cat says what their ritual item will do to banish their supernatural enemy and begins to make their best Cat meow. Once everyone is meowing, the supernatural enemy will try once again to get your Cat to succumb to Curiosity. One by one members of your coven will be tempted by the player to their right, in the order players introduced their ritual items. If your Cat fails, you can use your Arcane Power. If you have already used your Arcane Power, you can use your ritual item and reroll. If you fail that roll, or you do not have a ritual object, you are distracted. A least two members of the coven must remain undistracted in order for the supernatural threats to be defeated.

ENDING THE GAME

If your Cats succeed, go around the table and describe your enemy's defeat. If they fail, narrate the consequences of your enemy's success.

THE FINAL BATTLE IS HERE

NUMBER OF PLAYERS: 2 • PLAYING TIME: 1–2 hours • COMPLEXITY: ⚡⚡⚡
• YOU'LL NEED: Pen and paper, 1d6. • GOAL: Win the Final Battle and decide
the fate of your rival. • TAGS: Genre: Modern; Tone: Serious; Format:
GMless; Content: Competition, rivalry, tragedy BY TAKUMA OKADA

TO THE BITTER END

To the Bitter End is a game about a pair of rivals locked in an epic conflict. In this game they'll clash many times, over any setting that you can imagine: duels, cooking competitions, sports, racing, etc.

SETUP

First, you'll need the setting and tone of your game. Come up with a setting on your own, or choose something from the list of examples. Because this game can get dark, you should set the tone together before starting. A game of high school rivals might be more lighthearted than a game of two duelists with a deep grudge.

⚡ A bounty hunter and their target, a space pirate, who has led them on a merry chase across half the galaxy.

⚡ The top chef at a prestigious cooking academy and a transfer student who is rapidly climbing the ranks.

⚡ A master of the blade, hunting down the vampire who killed their mentor.

⚡ Two disciples of the greatest mage in the land.

Next, you'll need your rivals. To create your character, come up with a name, what your character looks like, and answers to the following core questions. Write all of your answers down.

⚡ What is a place that's important to you?

⚡ What is your dearest possession?

⚡ Whose respect must you earn?

⚡ Who can you trust?

These answers are your character's Cores. The pain of losing them is what intensifies your rivalry.

Finally, your character needs two abilities. Your abilities can be anything, but they should be tied to your setting. Come up with them on your own, or choose from the list of examples. You'll gain more abilities after each Rival Battle.

ABILITIES

⚡ Sword fighting

⚡ Acrobatics

⚡ Nimble fingers

⚡ Cooking

⚡ Super strength

⚡ Money

⚡ Photographic memory

⚡ A keen sense of smell

⚡ X-ray vision

⚡ Healing

⚡ Perfect pitch

⚡ Mathematics

⚡ Invisibility

⚡ Juggling

⚡ Punching

⚡ Singing

⚡ Empathy

⚡ Talking to animals

Gameplay

Now that the protagonist of the story is created, continue going around the table and have everyone work together to tell the full story of their Journey through the Desert. Each of you should draw on and include narration from the other players, as well as all the details you established in the first set of prompts. The following prompts can provide structure and guidance, but feel free to deviate from them or repeat ones as desired. Do not be afraid to spend time filling in details and fleshing out the story and character, but if you find yourself talking uninterrupted for extended periods of time, invite the other players to weigh in with suggestions and to finish off your thoughts for you.

PROMPTS

+ When I first set out into the Desert...
+ On my path I found...
+ When I went off my path...
+ Something changed when I...
+ The most remarkable moment was...
+ My Journey ended with...

THE HEART OF A STORY

With your story complete, go around the table one more time, and have each person explain the significance of the story to them. They should then distill it down into a one-sentence summary, a moral or guiding theme from the story. To you, this is the story's Heart. The Hearts can have similar themes, but should be distinct from one another.

THE SANDS' LAUGHTER SWALLOWS TIME

Like the Desert's shifting sands and changing landscapes, the details of a story evolve with every retelling; as the desert perseveres through time, so too does the Heart of a story.

As a group, take turns retelling parts of the story of the original journey. As you do this, alter, add, or remove elements of the story in order to better highlight the Heart you selected. The core of the story should stay the same, but feel free to change whatever details you'd like to emphasize what you see as the core theme. You can go back to the prompts for inspiration on the types of details you might add to the story.

The following guidelines can help guide your choice of what details to include or emphasize:

+ Is this detail fun to keep in? Does it support my Heart?
+ Does being more specific here heighten the impact? What about being vague?
+ How can I embellish and exaggerate without betraying the integrity of the story?
+ How can I rearrange details to make them all shine?

If you want a longer game, loop back up to "The Heart of a Story," with each player choosing new hearts for the next retelling. Use the already altered story as your base. You can keep doing this as many or as few times as you wish, further altering and shifting the story with each iteration, before progressing to the final section.

Ending the Game

You are all one traveler Journeying through the Desert. You must make it to the other side. As you crest another dune, expecting nothing but more sand to greet you, you see an image on the horizon. A snapshot of a past journey. A Mirage.

Work together to create a single scene that captures the essence of the story. This can be a specific scene that occurred in your narration or a thematic interpretation of the story.

Start by painting in broad strokes to convey the themes behind the story, and add details from there. Use the following prompts for guidance as needed:

+ What populates the landscape?
+ What colors make up the scene?
+ Are there textures or smells that stand out?
+ Which pieces are more focused?
+ Which pieces are less clear?
+ What feeling does it inspire?

Once that's done, have each person add one final detail to the illusion based on your Heart. It can be as small or large as you want, but it should leave a lasting impression on the scene.

As you rest atop the dune, the Mirage fades away. It was there for but a moment, but a moment was enough to glimpse the past, to see a long-lost journey, and to understand its Heart.

UNKINDNESS

A GAME ABOUT ADOLESCENT RAVENS

When a Raven reaches adolescence, they leave the nest... AND JOIN GANGS. Any gathering of ravens is called an UNKINDNESS, but TEENS wear the name well. In *Unkindness* you are a TEEN RAVEN. You live to cause MISCHIEF AND DESTRUCTION, and to experience EMOTION.

By James D'Amato

NUMBER OF PLAYERS: 3–6

PLAYING TIME: 1–2 hours

COMPLEXITY: ●●●●

YOU'LL NEED: 1d6, paper and pencils.

GOAL: To cause destruction and experience emotions as teen ravens.

TAGS:
• GENRE—Animals • TONE—Funny
• FORMAT—Rotating • CONTENT—Teenaged angst, risky behavior, social pressure, death

SETUP

Adolescent ravens start the game with these stats:
Youth: 4   Feelings: 4   Maturity: 0

ROLL A 1D6 TO SEW YOUR ADOLESCENT CHAOS:

Roll YOUTH for theft, moving fast, and avoiding danger.

Roll FEELINGS for breaking things, attacking enemies, and being a nuisance.

Roll maturity NEVER—maturity is boring and useless to adolescent ravens.

ROLL 1D6 TO GET A POWER:

⚀ **Mimicry:** perfectly re-create sounds in your environment, even human speech

⚁ **Loudness:** the ability to be extremely loud

⚂ **Tools:** using simple tools like sticks and rocks

⚃ **Memory:** the ability to recognize patterns and learn to avoid past mistakes

⚄ **Portent:** the ability to be a foul omen

⚅ **Wolves:** you are friends with some wolves

If you make a roll incorporating your POWER, you may choose to roll again once if you are not satisfied with your first result.

CHOOSE SOMETHING TO HATE:

Owls, cars, windows, old memes, capitalism

CHOOSE AN INSECURITY:

Wingspan, beak, athleticism, size, accomplishments, knowledge of nineteenth-century literature

NAME YOUR RAVEN:

If you need help, choose from this list: Mordechai, Shriek, Lilith, Shadow, Knife, Allen, Carol, Goblin, Vape, Lucifer, Asmodeus

GAMEPLAY

There are two phases to *Unkindness*; the first is Mischief and Destruction. Each round, a new member of the Unkindness chooses a goal for the group to pursue like:

• Steal something shiny   • Get into trash
• Mess with an owl   • Settle a score

If you have trouble selecting someone to choose a goal, pick whoever does the best 'CAW!'

Once a player chooses a goal, the rest of the group will create obstacles. Each player controls the obstacle they create and must describe how it vexes the Unkindness in pursuit of their goal. Obstacles can be physical dangers—like a human with a rake—or emotional like an argument within the Unkindness. Players take turns describing how their raven pursues the goal. Players in control of obstacles should describe how their obstacle gets in the way. To circumvent obstacles, ravens must roll.

All ravens roll against Youth or Feelings. Based on what you want to do, choose the most appropriate stat and roll a d6. If you roll under or equal your stat, you succeed, and you must describe your success. If you roll over your stat, you fail, and the player controlling the obstacle decides how things get more complicated.

If a Raven fails two rolls while causing Mischief and Destruction, they gain an Emotional Condition. Their Youth temporarily decreases by 1, and their Feelings increase by 1. Choose an emotion to inform your role-play:

- Anger
- Jealousy
- Depression
- Infatuation
- Existential Dread
- Joie de Vivre

If a Raven fails three rolls in one round of Mischief and Destruction, they might die. After three failed rolls, any event that could potentially kill you, does. Every member of the Unkindness must agree that a situation is lethal in order for this to happen. When a raven dies, everyone gains 1 point of Maturity.

Players can go around and take as many turns as needed to accomplish the goal. Mischief and Destruction ends once the player who picked the goal feels it has been accomplished or decides it 'sucks now.' After Mischief and Destruction, the Unkindness must Experience Emotion.

EXPERIENCE EMOTION

After adolescent ravens cause havoc, they must sort through the powerful emotions of youth. Each raven gets a turn to explore their feelings. Most emotional scenes are punctuated by a chorus of CAWs. When you feel a scene has reached its emotional height, or when prompted, CAW like a big noisy trash bird. Unless it is a romance scene, the rest of the group should join you.

The Unkindness Experiences Emotion doing one of the following activities:

BATHING:
Splashing around in a puddle or basin

EATING TRASH:
Beaking down on some good garbage

ANTING:
Rolling around in an anthill because it feels good

WATCHING SOMETHING BURN:
Just idly observing fire

After establishing your activity, work as a group to describe your location. Once everyone understands where they are, each player chooses to Rant, Rave, or Romance.

RANT Your emotions are overwhelming, and you need to share them or they will destroy you. Pick another raven and talk about your Emotional Condition. Discuss it until you feel you have learned a lesson and you both gain Maturity. Or you become so frustrated you have to CAW. No matter what, ranting will clear an Emotional Condition, returning your stats to normal.

RAVE You just did something rad, and the others have to know. Tell the group about what you did and why it makes you cool. Once you finish, slap your hand on the table and look at your Unkindness. They can either Validate you by erupting in a chorus of CAWs or Reject you by remaining silent. If you are Validated, you can select a new Power to use once in the next round. If you are Rejected, you gain a point of Maturity as you realize your actions were foolish.

ROMANCE Choose another raven in your Unkindness and attempt to Romance them by doing a cool stunt, offering a gift, or reciting a poem (we suggest selections from Edgar Allan Poe). Describe your effort to Romance the other bird. Once you have finished, the other player must CAW. Based on your Insecurity, decide if you think their CAW was Affirming or Mocking. If it was Affirming, the bird who was courted gains Maturity. If it was Mocking, you gain Maturity.

Once every player has Experienced Emotion, choose a raven to pick a new goal for Mischief and Destruction.

ENDING THE GAME

If Maturity becomes your highest stat, you grow up. If two ravens in your Unkindness grow up, they become adults and mate for life. They win the game, but everyone else is pretty sure they actually lost.

VAN GOGH'S EAR
The Game of Inadvisable Gifts

By Jenn Ellis and Keith Baker

What's the worst gift you can give to someone you care about? In *Van Gogh's Ear*, players craft competing tales of tragedy driven by thoughtful—and terrible—gifts, like Van Gogh's ear.

Setup

Before making characters, work with the other players to define the time and place of your story. Choose an option from the following table or make up your own. The setting will inform your choices in making your characters and relationships and will provide some sense of what gifts are possible.

Number of players: 2–5

Playing time: Under an hour

Complexity: ■ ■ □ □ □

You'll need: Standard deck of playing cards with jokers removed.

Goal: Give a gift to a fellow player that is both considerate for them and tragic for you.

Tags: Genre: Comedy | Tone: Funny | Format: GMless | Content: Cruel dramatic irony, cringingly terrible choices

Card	Role	Defining Trait	Loves	Prized Possession
Ace	Doctor	Vain	Themselves	Clothing or Jewelry
2	Artist	Penniless	Food	Music Collection or Instrument
3	Musician	Extroverted	Parties	Physical Attribute (Hair, Muscles)
4	Laborer	Shy	Animals	Artwork (Portrait, Sculpture)
5	Actor	Wealthy	Travel	Literature (Book, Letter, Poem)
6	Scientist or Academic	Haunted	Music	Tool (Hammer, Pen, Computer)
7	Soldier	Moody	Show Business	Weapon
8	Therapist	Miserly	The Simple Life	Child
9	Housekeeper	Compassionate	Art	Pet
10	Assistant	Generous	Fashion	Toy
Jack	Magician	Vengeful	Poetry or Literature	Memento (Photo, Souvenir)
Queen	Sophisticate or Socialite	Absent-Minded	Romance	Vehicle (Car, Boat, Carriage)
King	Executive or Leader	Famous	Thrills or Risk	Property (House, Land)

Gameplay

The game is divided into four turns, each turn corresponding to one season out of the year. During each season, each player will tell the others a short story about something that happens to the Meskarr people—either a specific person, a group of people, or the entire society as a whole. In subsequent seasons, you can decide to switch to other characters or groups of characters; you don't have to continue with the same thread you started before. This game is about a snapshot of their lives, not necessarily a thorough narrative with a particular cast. Just pick what feels right and go.

As you are telling your story, you and the other players will begin to draw a tattoo on part of your body that symbolizes the story you're telling this turn. Anyone can start drawing; anyone can add anything. The entire sequence is improvised. The tattoo can be an obvious form or something more abstract, but no single player gets to decide entirely what it is. Draw and add details until the story ends. When a player is finished for a turn, everyone should stop and admire what they've done.

Continue taking turns until everyone has gone. Note that the season has thus ended and a new one begins, and take turns all over again.

If you're stuck for ideas for stories or characters, consider the following list of fiction prompts. Use, change, or disregard as suits your play:

- A fisherman who catches food for the hunting lodge with a ceremonial sword.
- The festival of growth, where trees are planted in meaningful formations on the outskirts of the village.
- A battle between sisters, near the shore, as ships approach.
- The priest and his chest of scrolls, on each one a dream of childbirth recorded, good omens.
- The dirt trails where fireflies gather and the love stories young genderless bards tell there.
- A storm that approaches but curiously moves around the village, never through.

Ending the Game

The game ends once the fourth turn, Winter, leaves us and everyone has given their final story. Consider cleaning up together, or else go home and do it separately. The ink may vanish, but the stories will remain.

WILD ROVERS

Tricks, Trials, Treats, and Finding Your Way Back Home

By Shanna Germain

Number of players: 4–8

Playing time: 20–35 minutes

Complexity: 🐾 🐾 🐾 🐾

You'll need: Stack of index cards, writing utensils.

Goal: To find your way home together.

Tags: Genre: Animals **Tone:** Adventurous **Format:** GMless **Content:** Family, hopeful, sweet

You play a group of dogs who have gotten lost out in the world. You must work together to overcome obstacles and find your way back home to your beloved owner.

Setup

Choose one person to be the dogs' owner. The owner should write their name on one side of an index card (that the other players can see). On the other side (keeping it private) they should write a Treat they have up their sleeve to help their dogs find their way home (such as a dog whistle, a strong-smelling snack, or a drone that hovers over the dogs and tells them what good dogs they are). If there are six or more players, the owner should write down two Treats.

Everyone else plays one of the dogs who have lost their way home. To create their characters, players will need to decide the following:

🦴 **Name**

🦴 **Gender**

🦴 **Breed**

🦴 **Appearance**

🦴 **Best Trick:** One thing they're great at

🦴 **Worst Trick:** One thing they're horrible at

For example, one player might decide to play Bingo the St. Bernard, whose Best Trick is helping their friends and whose Worst Trick is ignoring squirrels. Another player might play Elsie the Spotted Mutt, whose Best Trick is rolling over and whose Worst Trick is "leave it." The weirder and more unique the dog's Best and Worst Tricks are, the more fun the game will be. Players should each write their name, breed/type/appearance, and gender pronouns on one side of an index card, large enough so that everyone at the table can read them. On the other side, players should secretly write down their character's Best and Worst Tricks. (Don't share these yet!)

Once character creation is finished, each player takes a new index card. On their card, they write down one Trial. A Trial is a hurdle, obstacle, or other difficulty that prevents the dogs from finding their way back home. It could be a hot dog stand that smells so enticing it's hard to ignore. Or a dogcatcher who's been chasing after the dogs since they got lost and has now caught up with them. The more outlandish the Trial, the more fun it will be to try to overcome it. Trials should be kept secret from the other players and, ideally, shouldn't be based on their own character's Tricks.

Once the Trials are finished, hand them all over to the owner, who shuffles them (without looking at them) and spreads them out face-down on the table.

Gameplay

The game begins with the owner telling a short story of how the dogs got lost—perhaps a mail carrier left the gate open, or an ice cream truck went by and everyone chased after it, or maybe they all got scared by some fireworks. The story can be as elaborate, funny, scary, or interesting as the owner wants to make it.

When the story is finished, the owner turns over one of the Trial cards. This is the first obstacle that the dogs will encounter when trying to find their way home. Each Trial card is a story opportunity, and the players must work together to create the story of how the dogs will succeed. To find their way back home, the dogs will need to overcome all of the Trials.

Here's the trick, however: In order to win and get through all of the Trials, each dog must use both their Best Trick and their Worst Trick once and only once in the game (but not in the same Trial). Don't be afraid to get creative and elaborate on how each dog's Tricks will work to help the plan succeed. If everyone in the group deems that the plan works, then the dogs overcome that Trial and get one step closer to home. If at any point a plan seems impossible or overly dangerous, the owner can choose to use their Treat as part of the story to help the dogs succeed.

Ending the Game

If the players overcome all of the Trials while using their Tricks and Treats, then the dogs find their way home, where their owner greets them happily and rewards them with belly rubs and scritches.

WITH SWORD HEAVY IN HAND
LOVE AND REGRET AT THE TIP OF A BLADE
By Kienna Shaw

NUMBER OF PLAYERS: 1

PLAYING TIME: 30 minutes–1 hour

COMPLEXITY: 1

YOU'LL NEED: Paper, writing utensils, and 1d6.

GOAL: Finish your journey and make your decision.

TAGS:

Genre: Fantasy

Tone: Serious

Format: GMless

Content: Revenge, nostalgia, regret

This is a game about embarking on a journey of remembrance and making a fateful choice.

Long ago you had a companion, and together you were two warriors invincible with your swords. But something broke the two of you apart, and your paths were separated…until now. You have been tasked to stop your former companion and their plans for destruction—even if they must fall to your blade. What places will you pass through on your journey to find them? What memories will you unearth? And what will you say and do when you finally see them again?

SETUP

First, create your character by answering the following questions:

- *What is your name?*
- *What is the significance of the sword you carry?*
- *What personal stake do you have in this mission?*
- *Why do you still care for your former companion?*

Next, create your former companion by answering the following questions:

- *What is their name?*
- *What relationship did you have with them?*
- *Why did your relationship break apart?*
- *Why must they be stopped?*

GAMEPLAY

Your journey will take you through six different locations. Roll a d6 or pick one of the locations from the following list (you may reroll any duplicates).

1. A valley of ever-blooming flowers
2. A city long abandoned to shadows
3. A lake reflecting moonlight
4. A cliffside facing the sunset
5. A forest showering leaves like rain
6. A desert glittering under the sun

Each of these locations evokes a memory of your time with your former companion. Roll a d6 or pick one of the memories from the following list (you may reroll any duplicates).

1. A pact, promise, or debt
2. A moment of betrayal, deception, or bad faith
3. A fight, danger, or threat
4. A moment of vulnerability, openness, or intimacy
5. A doubt, fear, or regret
6. A moment in a home, sanctuary, or hideout

After rolling for a location and a memory, choose and answer two of the questions from the following list.

- *Why are you reminded of your former companion here?*
- *What emotion rises in your heart as you remember?*
- *What sensation (sight/smell/sound/taste/touch) reminds you of the days now lost?*
- *Why do you regret coming here?*
- *What here comforts you?*
- *What here makes you uneasy?*
- *Why does your sword feel especially heavy here?*
- *What token do you take with you?*
- *What thought lingers with you?*
- *Why do you feel compelled to continue forward?*

Write down your answers and thoughts in a short letter to share with your former companion when you finally meet again. Repeat this process until you have completed six letters.

ENDING THE GAME

When you finish the sixth letter, answer the following questions:

- *Where do you find your former companion waiting for you?*
- *What do you feel upon seeing them?*
- *What memory of your journey and your relationship do you share with them?*
- *Do you raise your blade?*

A Game about Making It Big Exactly Once, and the People along the Way

WONDERS

BY ALEX FLANIGAN

Number of players: 3–6

Playing time: 30–90 minutes

Complexity: ♪♪♪♪

You'll need: 1d6, paper, pen.

Goal: To write the song that makes you famous, and destroy the band in the process.

Tags:

Genre—Modern; Tone—Funny; Format—GMless;

Content—Arguments, improv, role-playing challenges

You are a group of best friends making the best music the world has ever known—they just don't know it *yet*. But it's only going to take one perfect song to get everyone to stand up and take notice, and then your career will open wide in front of you. Besides, you all work so perfectly together. How hard can it be?

SETUP

Choose one musician from each category (or roll a d6) to build your individual character:

Pick your **instrument**:

- ⚀ Lead guitar
- ⚁ Vocals
- ⚂ Drums
- ⚃ Bass
- ⚄ Keys
- ⚅ Rhythm guitar

Pick your **truth**:

- ⚀ Honoring the Greats
- ⚁ Making history
- ⚂ Scoring fans
- ⚃ Getting out of this town
- ⚄ Changing the world
- ⚅ Having a good time

Choose your **stage name**:

Together, decide on your **band name**:

Use the following list to choose your **sound**:

- ⚀ 50s rock
- ⚁ 60s pop
- ⚂ 70s folk
- ⚃ 80s ballads
- ⚄ 90s grunge
- ⚅ 00s pop-punk

Somewhere—scrap of paper, your arm, the side of your Converse shoes, the drummer's T-shirt—keep a space for tally marks. This will be where you mark **Tension** later on. Tension is a personal score that you can choose to keep visible to the group or keep secret from everyone else.

GAMEPLAY

You all have to work together to write the big hit you know you have inside you. But communication is hard. Each member of your band has a distinct personality quirk that makes them impossible to work with.

Lead guitarist: can only speak in "I" statements

Vocalist: can't answer questions directly

Drummer: taps loudly and continuously on nearby surfaces while talking

Bassist: can't speak unless spoken to

Keyboardist: can't approve another person's phrase without first changing a word

Rhythm guitarist: can't use words more than two syllables long

Without consulting anyone else in the band, decide on your own personal **Mantra**. This is the message you want your music to convey, the charge you want to share with the world. It will help guide your writing process. It could be something simple, like "Love will save the world" or "Live fast, die young, party hard," or it could be something more specific and complicated, like "Jenny Deacon broke my heart in the third grade and I've never forgotten the smell of her cherry lip balm" or "Horses are really freaky and we can all agree on that, right?" A good rule of thumb is that lyrics that align with your Mantra will get your seal of approval, and lyrics that don't will be ones you disagree with. More specific Mantras will lead to a more challenging game, but they will also yield more entertaining lyrics!

MAKING MAGIC

Pull out a blank piece of paper. Try to write twenty-four lines of song lyrics by collaborating out loud. A lyric becomes locked in once a simple majority of the band agrees on it. If you dissent with a locked-in lyric, or your opinion isn't asked, mark a point of Tension. After 3 points of Tension, you leave the band, preferably by flipping something over and accusing someone of selling out. Immediately replace yourself with a new character and continue gameplay.

ENDING THE GAME

The game is won if you complete all twenty-four lyrics with at least one original band member remaining.

You never make another hit together. End the game by describing where each member of the band, past and present, ended up. Together, answer the following questions:

Was it worth it?

Would you do it all again?

YOU WERE NEVER REALLY HERE

A Surreal Ghost Story Game

By Ben Chong

Number of players: 3–5

Playing time: 1–2 hours

Complexity: ▮▮▮▯

You'll need:

Index cards, scissors, some string, 1d6, 1d10, writing utensils, cork board to pin/magnetize string to.

Goal:

Solve the mystery and find the Ghost.

Tags:

Genre: Horror
Tone: Scary
Format: GMless
Content: Web building, spooky

There is a Ghost among you. Long ago, they died without a single soul knowing—their yearning turned you Haunted. Now, you've come together to uncover it all. What dark secrets will you find? Why are you Haunted? Who is the Ghost? Solve the mystery, find the Ghost, or risk being Haunted forever.

SETUP

First, create the Haunted. Each player is a Haunted, victims of the Ghost's yearning. Before playing, the Haunted must answer the following:

- Who are you? (name/look/pronouns)

- How would you describe yourself in two words or less?

The Haunted notes down their details on an index card. The index cards are placed in front of them for all to see.

Establish Connections

Taking turns, each Haunted must establish one connection with another Haunted. This may be positive or negative. The Haunted involved summarize the connections on their respective index cards. They then tie a single string between each other's wrists to represent their connection. In between the Haunted, place an index card for the Ghost. Once this is done and every Haunted has established a connection, you're ready to play the game.

GAMEPLAY

You Were Never Really Here is played in four chapters. In each, the Haunted take turns choosing their own prompts to play a scene. The Haunted play and narrate their pursuits to uncover the mystery. In each scene, the Haunted must involve at least one or more of their connections, and may involve the Ghost. The Haunted may create new elements such as places, people, or objects for the scene.

When it feels right, end the scene and cross the prompt off for everyone. Then, each of the Haunted take turns to perform one of the following:

- **Create a Connection:** Tie a string between two of the Haunted involved. *Relationships deepen.*

- **Remove a Connection:** Cut the string between two of the Haunted involved. *Relationships die.*

- **Create a Clue:** Create a card to highlight an element from the scene. *A new lead is found.*

- **Remove a Clue:** Remove a card for an element from the scene. *An old lead is disproven.*

The Haunted who created the scene must always create a connection. If a Haunted has only one connection left, or if there are no clues, only new connections and clues can be created.

Focus on the surreal, strange, and spooky. Improvise, plan together, and chase interesting threads. Every scene should always advance the mystery.

Once every prompt is crossed off, the Haunted continue to the next chapter and repeat.

Chapter 1: Introductions

The Haunted encounter strange things
and find each other. Roll a d6.

- Unexpected meetings keep happening. *How is the Ghost doing this?*

- A bad omen is witnessed. *What does it represent?*

- Weird sights manifest in dreams. *What does it communicate?*

- Unknown faces appear out of nowhere. *Who are they?*

- A forgotten tale is brought up. *What does it remind you of?*

- Weird artifacts are found in clutter, trash, between rocks. *Where do these tell you to go?*

Chapter 2: Escalations

The Haunted invite the strange and dangerous,
and the mystery drags them deeper. Roll a d10 to
determine which of the following occurs:

- 1 A vital resource is tainted. *What does it represent for the Ghost?*

- 2 Mysterious wounds appear. *What is their nature?*

- 3 Gaps of time go missing. *What happens in between?*

- 4 The Ghost exerts control. *What does it demand?*

- 5 A betrayal is discovered among you. *How is the Ghost involved?*

- 6 An ancient message is deciphered. *What instructions does it give?*

- 7 A dark, damning secret is spilled. *What illusion does it shatter?*

- 8 The world twists and bends on itself. *Why does the Ghost separate you?*

- 9 A dangerous ritual is found. *How will it only make things worse?*

- 0 Someone is lost and returned. *How do they come back different?*

Chapter 3: Revelations

The Haunted solve the mystery and uncover
the Ghost among them.
Look at each other: Who is the least connected?
They are the Ghost.

As the Haunted, answer:

1. How did the Ghost die? *How are you involved?*

2. How were they forgotten? *Who left them there?*

3. How can they move on? *What do you do together for the Ghost?*

As the Ghost, answer:

1. How did you truly die? *What did they miss?*

2. How did you haunt them? *What did they see if you were never really there?*

3. How will you move on? *What do you do for them in return?*

The Mystery is solved. The Ghost is uncovered. You are no longer Haunted. Cut your strings and discard everything.

ENDING THE GAME

Together, discuss what happens to the Haunted.
How have they changed? Where will they go? What will they do?

Appendix A

GAMES BY GENRE

FANTASY

Absolution in Brass

The Agony of Elves

Broken Swords and Twisted Trails

Gnomesteaders

A Green Hour

Mythology

Swords by Starlight

Truth in the Mirage

What Our Bodies Tell Us

With Sword Heavy in Hand

SCIENCE FICTION

Breaking Rank

Dead Planet

Distant Stars

Doomed Stars

Event Planning in Zero G

Hammer of the Earth

Pyrewaltz

COMEDY

Break Room

Pig at a Wedding

Van Gogh's Ear

HORROR

It Wants Souls

Lycantree

You Were Never Really Here

MODERN

Annedale-by-Sea

Going Dark

Heartbeats

A Machine Larger Than You

Neural Splinters

Object Kilo

On All Frequencies

A Pleasant Evening

Summer Break!

To the Bitter End

Wonders

SPORTS

Post-Match Interview

Super Overtime

ANIMALS

Hero Dog Saves Town

Tales from the Corner Coven

Unkindness

Wild Rovers

Appendix B

GAMES BY COMPLEXITY

COMPLEXITY: 1

Event Planning in Zero G

Hero Dog Saves Town

A Pleasant Evening

Post-Match Interview

Swords by Starlight

Van Gogh's Ear

What Our Bodies Tell Us

With Sword Heavy in Hand

COMPLEXITY: 2

The Agony of Elves

Break Room

Breaking Rank

Doomed Stars

A Green Hour

Heartbeats

It Wants Souls

Lycantree

Neural Splinters

Object Kilo

Pig at a Wedding

To the Bitter End

Unkindness

Wild Rovers

Wonders

COMPLEXITY: 3

Absolution in Brass

Annedale-by-Sea

Broken Swords and Twisted Trails

Distant Stars

Gnomesteaders

Going Dark

A Machine Larger Than You

On All Frequencies

Summer Break!

Super Overtime

Tales from the Corner Coven

Truth in the Mirage

You Were Never Really Here

COMPLEXITY: 4

Dead Planet

Hammer of the Earth

Mythology

Pyrewaltz

ABOUT THE AUTHORS

James D'Amato is the author of *The Ultimate RPG Character Backstory Guide* and *The Ultimate RPG Gameplay Guide*, as well as the creator and game master of *One Shot* podcast and *Campaign: Skyjacks* podcast dedicated to RPG gameplay. He trained at Second City and iO in Chicago in the art of improvisational comedy; he now uses that education to introduce new people to role-playing and incorporates improvisational storytelling techniques to create compelling and entertaining stories for RPG campaigns and one-shot adventures.

A game designer, writer, artist, and sneaker enthusiast born and raised in New Orleans and currently living in Durham, NC, **Omari Akil** has designed and published games independently since 2018 and seeks to continue pushing the limits of whom tabletop games can reach and the type of content they bring to the forefront. His premier board game, *Rap Godz*, connected hip-hop culture to board games in a way that has never been done before. He continues to explore game designs and themes that are linked to African diaspora and Afrofuturism in his quest to become a full-time gaming professional.

Amr Ammourazz is a writer, game designer, and podcaster who creates fiction to reflect Egyptian culture and the way it permeates throughout their perspective. Their games are designed to showcase how mechanics and narrative can work together to promote the same experience, while spanning the scope from emotionally intense to comic book–zany. By day, they yell at robots to move (a highly technical approach) and stare at numbers until they arrange themselves logically on a page. Sometimes, it even works!

Anna Anthropy is a game designer, educator, and thirtysomething teen witch. She is the author of seven books and too many games (many of which can be found at w.itch.io), and she teaches game design as DePaul University's Game Designer in Residence. She lives in Chicago with her familiar, a little black cat named Encyclopedia Frown.

Joey "Gnomedic" Barranco, of Chicago, is a game designer, broadcaster, and social media wizard. Recent collaborative storytelling work includes podcasts like *Rise of the Demigods* and streaming TTRPGs on Twitch.

Caitlynn Aura Belle (they/she/it) is a game designer, artist, and burlesque performer from Savannah, GA. Their game *A Real Game* won the Indie Groundbreaker Award for Game of the Year, and many of her works have appeared in podcasts and live streams. It has worked on many indie games during their *Kickstarter* runs, and also cowrote *Singularity: A Transhumanist Dating LARP*, with Ginger Goat. It can be found on *Twitter* at @auracait.

Sharang Biswas is a writer, interactive theater maker, game designer, and artist. He has published games through Pelgrane Press, Cryptozoic Entertainment, *Rolled & Told* magazine, and *sub-Q* magazine, and created large-scale games for clients such as the Ford Foundation and the Museum of the Moving Image. He won the Dark Horse Award at the International Festival of Independent Games (IndieCade), and twice won the Indie Game Developer Network (IGDN) Most Innovative Game award. Sharang has taught and lectured on game design and interactive art at numerous institutions, including Dartmouth College, New York University, Bard College, and Fordham University. His website is https://sharangbiswas.myportfolio.com, and you can find him on *Twitter* at @SharangBiswas, and itch.io at https://astrolingus.itch.io/.

Nathan Blades is an androgynous android game show host from the future who works in broadcasting when not rolling dice. They produce a mixed-system actual play podcast called *The Talent Agency*, and have several written RPG works to their name, including *The Queer Cyberpunk's Guide to Tabletop RPGs*.

Ben Chong, also known as Flowers, is a nonbinary, bi Malaysian-Chinese tabletop game designer making games about intimacy, relationships, tough conversations, and everyday magic. Their works are inspired by romance, surrealism, and horror with a Southeast Asian bent. Ben imagines deep, emotional worlds to touch the hearts of players. Under the name Swords and Flowers, Ben self-publishes; runs workshops, mentorship programs, and community events; and collaborates on international projects. They currently lecture for game design in UOW Malaysia KDU's Bachelor of Game Development (Hons).

Jay Dragon is a lyrical and narrative game designer in the Hudson Valley who writes games about communities, queerness, monstrosity, found family, and hope. Jay can often be found sitting by the river, exploring the woods, and teaching kids about flower crowns.

Jenn Ellis and **Keith Baker** pursue their love of bringing people together through story-telling through their company Twogether Studios, with games ranging from the light-hearted *Action Cats!* to the RPG *Phoenix: Dawn Command*. Their latest game, *The Adventure Zone: Bureau of Balance*, lets any group of players follow in the footsteps of the McElroy family to create a fun fantasy adventure. Outside of Twogether Studios, Keith is also known for creating the storytelling card game Gloom and the Eberron Campaign Setting for *Dungeons & Dragons*.

Armed with a very niche college degree and a handful of semi-notable playwriting credits, **Alex Flanigan** entered the world of RPG writing the same way she entered most other pursuits: underprepared, overwhelmed, and highly caffeinated. She lives in Virginia—the boring one without all the best mountains—with one fiancé and one extremely good dog, and can be found every week on *A Horror Borealis* and *The Cryptid Keeper* wherever it is that you get your podcasts.

Shanna Germain is a writer, editor, and game designer, as well as the co-owner of Monte Cook Games. Her work includes *No Thank You, Evil!*, *Numenera*, *Invisible Sun*, *Predation*, *The Poison Eater*, *Tomorrow's Bones*, and the forthcoming fairy tale game *We Are All Mad Here*. Visit her online at ShannaGermain.com.

Anil Godigamuwe is a corporate wordslinger and cat shepherd (aka Communications Officer & Community Manager) for Rusty Quill, an independent entertainment company and podcast network. A long-time TRPG player who started with AD&D, he's now collaborating on game design and working on his own game hacks. He's also a variety streamer and host on the Rusty Quill Twitch channel. As a poet, Anil has performed at various conventions and Vogon slams. His work has been included in *Poems for the Queer Revolution* (2015) and the role-playing game *Lovecraftesque* (2016). You can find him managing the various Rusty Quill online presences (@therustyquill) or on his own *Twitter* (@godigumdrop).

Aly Grauer is an author, actor, and podcaster based in Orlando, FL. She is a performer in theme parks and has published several short stories and at least one novel. She also teaches dialect lessons for theater and gaming. Her first game, *Sidewalkia!*, was a winner of the 200 Word RPG Challenge in 2018.

Adira Slattery is a game designer, podcaster, and zinester. She lives in Chicagoland with her spouse and two amazing cats. Always up for a new experience or a weird mechanic, Adira loves to exist in the experimental edges of tabletop and LARP. She makes games that explore intimacy, optimism, futility, and both queer and Jewish themes. Adira is also a member of the lyric games movement, focusing on emotional experiences and poetic expression through her design. Her self-published zines and games can be downloaded from adira.itch.io.

Pidj Sorensen is an avid game master, writer, and player of role-playing games, having begun in high school. Many TTRPGs (tabletop role-playing games) feature very narrow concepts—a medieval European fantasy with violent yet somehow noble adventurers slaying "monsters," for example. While those games can be fun, they're pervasive. Pidj tries to provide alternate frameworks that allow for different narratives: nonviolence, a centering of indigenous values, games that are inclusive and thoughtful in their fun. In designing player-first mechanics, they draw on their psychology and computer science background. Pidj has a lot of hope for the future of TTRPGs—it is such an exciting time to design and play!

Soup (they/them) is a nonbinary Korean-American indie tabletop game designer who has been self-publishing since 2018. They started designing for a course on experimental tabletop game design in university and never really stopped. They mostly sit on a hoard of near-finished games waiting for formatting like some kind of esoteric game-developing hermit growing mushrooms deep in the forest. Soup's design is largely influenced by the unhealthy amount of anime that they watch.

PYREWALTZ character sheets

MECH: _____ ①   _____ ⑦

FINISHING MOVE: _____ ② _____ ③ : _____ ④ _____ ⑤ _____ ⑥

A:

B:

C:

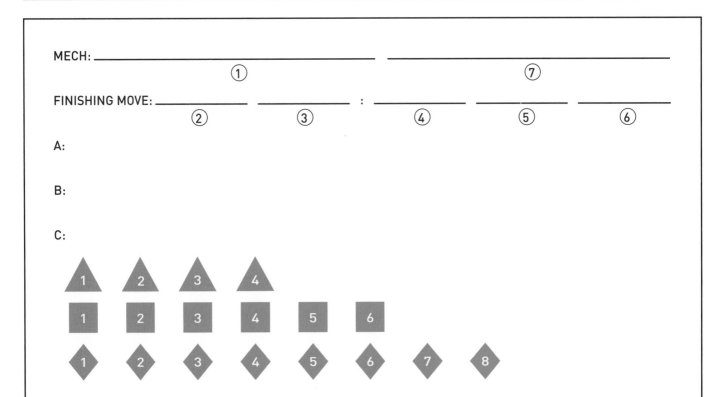

MECH: _____ ①   _____ ⑦

FINISHING MOVE: _____ ② _____ ③ : _____ ④ _____ ⑤ _____ ⑥

A:

B:

C:

PYREWALTZ character sheets

MECH: _____ _____
　　　　　　　　①　　　　　　　　　　　　　　⑦

FINISHING MOVE: _____ _____ : _____ _____ _____
　　　　　　　　②　　　　　③　　　　④　　　　⑤　　　　⑥

A:

B:

C:

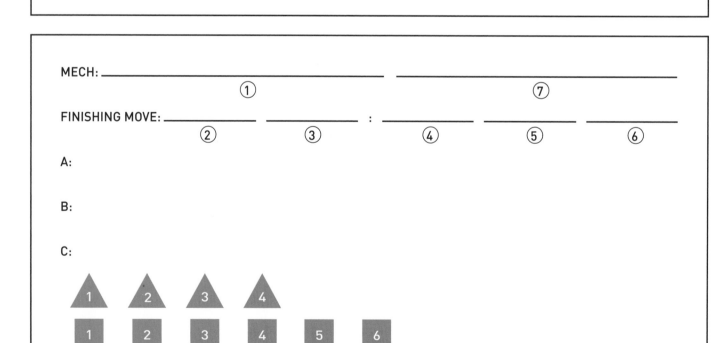

MECH: _____ _____
　　　　　　　　①　　　　　　　　　　　　　　⑦

FINISHING MOVE: _____ _____ : _____ _____ _____
　　　　　　　　②　　　　　③　　　　④　　　　⑤　　　　⑥

A:

B:

C:

TAKE YOUR GAMEPLAY TO THE NEXT LEVEL!

PICK UP OR DOWNLOAD YOUR COPIES TODAY!

Do you have a favorite toy?

A favorite superhero?

A favorite teddy?

Yippee!

We all have favorite things.

These things are worth more to us, and we treat them better, because they are our favorites!

It's fine to play favorites like this...

... unless we play favorites
            with people.

What happens if we play favorites with some people and treat others not so well?

It makes those not-well-treated people feel sad and lonely and like they are worth less than others. It's a big problem.

This isn't a new problem. It's a very old problem. And it's such a big problem that a long time ago, in the Bible, when a church leader called James wrote to some Christians, he wanted them to think hard about it.

So he told them a story...

Imagine (wrote James) that it's a Sunday and you're all in church. And then, just before the service starts, in walks a really rich man, wearing a gold ring and fine clothing (because that's what rich people wore in James's time).

Here's what they did...

Then imagine (wrote James) that a poor man walks in, wearing shabby clothes (because that's what people who had very little money wore in James's time).

Here's what they did...

This church was playing favorites based on how much money people had. They gave a big welcome to people who had lots, but they had no welcome for people who had little.

But (wrote James) rich people weren't better than poorer people. Some of those rich people were being mean to Christians. Some of them did not love Jesus.

And although poor people did not have much money, many of them did love Jesus. They had treasures upon treasures and a big wide welcome waiting for them in heaven.

So (James wrote), don't play favorites. Instead, choose to love.

Like those churches, we might treat people better because they have more money or nicer clothes. And we can play favorites with people in other ways, too.

We can play favorites because of the color of someone's skin...

... or because of someone's physical abilities...

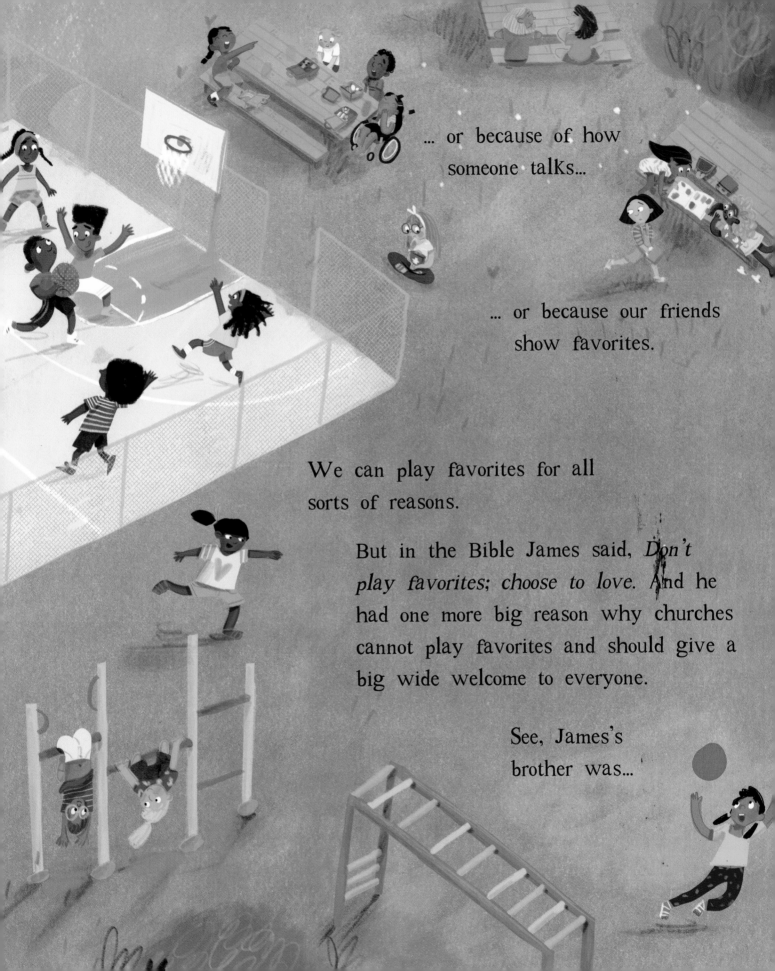

... or because of how someone talks...

... or because our friends show favorites.

We can play favorites for all sorts of reasons.

But in the Bible James said, *Don't play favorites; choose to love.* And he had one more big reason why churches cannot play favorites and should give a big wide welcome to everyone.

See, James's brother was...

Jesus! James had grown up seeing Jesus every day!

He knew that Jesus was perfect in every way. Jesus did everything right. When Jesus, the Son of God, walked on the earth as a man, he talked to all sorts of people.

Jesus talked to people who had fancy clothes.
Jesus talked to people who had shabby clothes.

Jesus talked to people who had darker skin.
Jesus talked to people who had lighter skin.

Jesus talked to very sick people.

Jesus talked to people who everyone else chose not to talk to.

Why?

Because Jesus loves all people.

He didn't only want to be friends with rich people, or clever people, or famous people. Jesus knew that everyone was in trouble because they had decided not to live with God as their Savior and Friend. Jesus knew that everyone needed him to rescue them.

Jesus didn't play favorites...

John 4 v 1-42

Jo...

Luke 7 v 36-50

Luke 5 v 12-16

Matthew 8 v 5-13

Luke 8 v 43-48

Mark 10 v 13-16

1-21

Mark 5 v 1-20

Luke 8 v 41-42, 49-55

Luke 13 v 10-17

Luke 19 v 1-10

Luke 5 v 1-11

... Jesus chose to LOVE!

In fact, Jesus loves people so much that he chose to die on the cross so that all people could be friends with him. Jesus welcomes as his friend anyone who asks to be his friend!

Rich people can be friends with Jesus.

Poor people can be friends with Jesus.

People whose bodies work different or look different can be friends with Jesus.

People who speak French or Korean or Spanish or Swahili or English can be friends with Jesus.

ALL WELCOME

And that means...

You can be friends
with Jesus, too!

NOT
BECAUSE

... you look great or
wear cool stuff

... you are good at sports

... you are smart

... you behave well

BUT
BECAUSE

Jesus chooses to love

y<u>ou</u>!

James says, *If you're friends with Jesus, be like Jesus.*
Jesus doesn't want you to play favorites with people.
He wants you to love people like he loves people.

And when you find that hard, you can always talk to him and ask him to help you — and he will!

Our churches should be big-wide-welcome places — places where there are no favorites, and everyone is loved.

You can be like Jesus wherever you are...

At school.

Playing sports.

At home.

In the park.

You can decide,

"I won't play favorites –
I will choose to love."

And most of all, you can remember that
Jesus doesn't play favorites. And that
means that, wherever you are and whoever
you are, Jesus loves YOU!

HOW DO WE KNOW ABOUT
THE BIG WIDE WELCOME?

You'll find the Bible passage at the heart of this book in James 2 v 1-26. In this powerful section in his letter to a 1st-century church, James challenges the church to repent of their sin of partiality (favoritism). When someone with wealth came into their midst, the church members would bring the rich person to a seat of honor and swoon over them, while a poor person would be treated in the opposite way and ignored. James spoke strongly against this treatment of people because God does not exercise partiality (Romans 2 v 11; Acts 10 v 34), and all those of us who love God are called to love our neighbor as ourselves (Mark 12 v 29-31).

James's rebuke is strong, but filled with good news. Since God isn't partial, anyone who believes in Jesus can know him and enjoy him forever! James's challenge is therefore also an invitation to all of us: to put away favoritism and to learn to love and enjoy each other — because we know that this is how God, in Jesus, loves us.